The
CLYDE ISLANDS
Arran, Bute and the Cumbraes

Pocket Visitors' Guide

John Gillham

ᴬQUESTA
Pocket Visitors' Guide

A QUESTA GUIDE

ISBN 1 898808 23 6

Questa Publishing, PO Box 520, Bamber Bridge, Preston, Lancashire PR5 8LF.

CONTENTS

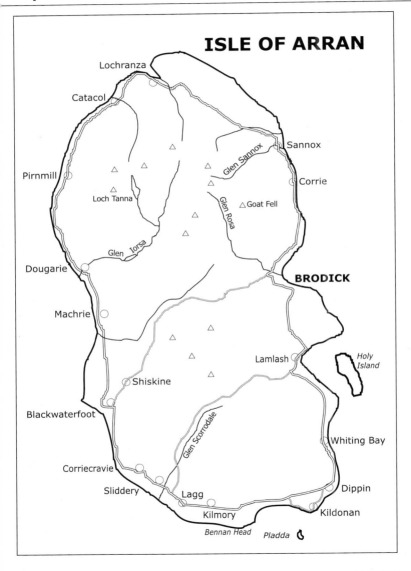

ISLE OF ARRAN

Lochranza

Catacol

Sannox

Glen Sannox

Pirnmill

Corrie

Loch Tanna

Glen Rosa

△Goat Fell

Glen Iorsa

Dougarie

BRODICK

Machrie

Lamlash

Holy Island

Shiskine

Blackwaterfoot

Glen Scorrodale

Whiting Bay

Corriecravie

Sliddery

Lagg

Dippin

Kilmory

Kildonan

Bennan Head   *Pladda*

Introduction

Scotland's sinuous southwest shorelines wrap themselves around the isles of Arran, Bute and the Cumbraes like a caring mother's arms, sheltering them from the harsh winds of the North. Here the River Clyde meets the sea: not the Clyde of shipping cranes and tenement buildings, but a wide and beautiful firth surrounded by the splendour of the heather hills of Cowal and Kintyre.

This was Buteshire, a place where ships were all-important, from the days when Viking longboats plundered the islands, to those when herring boats, Clyde cargo puffers, and steamships plied their trade on busy waters. Today, Arran and the Cumbraes are part of Ayrshire, while Bute belongs to Argyll. The herring boats sail no more, their place, but not their role, taken by the roll-on, roll-off ferries of Caledonian MacBrayne who bring the tourists to visit the islands in the firth.

Arran: the Isle of Peaks

Arran is a mountainous island: you can see that from the Ayrshire Coast, where the mountains take the form of a sleeping warrior. It is a beautiful and unspoilt island where the Highlands and the Lowlands meet; far enough across the water to be romantically remote, and near enough to be accessible – a 55-minute trip on CalMac's *MV Caledonian Isles* will see you driving off the slipway into Brodick.

The island measures 20 miles by 10 (32km by 16), and if you like lightning tours you can drive the 56-mile (90km) coast road in less than three hours. You'd manage to see all the pretty coastal villages and catch the very next ferry, but you'd miss the point, for Arran isn't renowned as 'Scotland in Miniature' for nothing. Though the equivalent of Glasgow's urban conurbations are missing, everything else is here. And while 90% of the population lives on or near the coast, the visitor who cares to explore can wander off into the heartland and experience a remoteness not hinted at by the map.

The Highlands of Arran, like those of the mainland, lie to the north. Here, the crystal streams of Glen Rosa and Glen Sannox are surrounded by the grandeur of serrated granite mountains that soar to Goatfell. The mountains crowd the coastline leaving little room for settlements. Those that do exist – Pirnmill, Sannox, Corrie and Catacol – huddle together on ribbon-like plains, facing the sea. Only little Lochranza has room to grow, but Lochranza has seen busier times and chooses these days to bask quietly, like the seals on shoreline rocks.

In the south the hills get lower, rounder and greener. Here, the rocks are replaced by heather, bracken and tussocky moor grass. Great sprucewoods have been planted, just as they have in Galloway and the Southern Uplands, and these, in turn, fall away to the small green fields, cliffs and bluffs, and the rugged rocky coastline of the south.

Bute

While Arran is mountainous, nearby Bute has only low hills. Indeed, when looking from mainland Argyll you can see the more distant mountains of Arran beyond and mistake them for a part of Bute.

The island measures a mere 15 miles by 5 (24km by 8). In the north it's separated from the mainland peninsular of Cowal by two narrow stretches of water, the Kyles of Bute. A small CalMac ferry sails across the eastern Kyle, linking Rhobodach (Rubha a' Bhodaich) with Colintraive on the mainland. This indeed would make a beautiful approach for those living in the North and those with time to first cross on the ferry from Gourock to Dunoon. The forests, the heathered hills and complex coastline of Cowal make a lovely start to your journey. Many travellers choose to take the direct half-hour ferry from Wemyss Bay on the Strathclyde Coast to Rothesay.

Rothesay is a lively place, and you can see by its four-storey Georgian and Victorian buildings that it was once an important place. While all of Arran is rural, here in Rothesay is a bustling, urban community. Most of the island's population lives here and many work here, too. Rothesay also has a proud history, and lots of it. It's a Royal Burgh, a charter bestowed on it by James I of Scotland; there's a 14th-century moated castle once occupied by the Royal Stewarts; and there's as fine an example of Art Nouveau style of architecture – the glass and steelwork Winter Garden – as you'll see in all Scotland. A regular caller to the harbour here is the paddle steamer, *Waverley*, a romantic two-chimneyed ship, bringing to mind bygone days of steam.

Three miles south of Rothesay, Mount Stuart is Bute's star attraction. If you do nothing else on the island, visit Mount Stuart, home to the Stuarts of Bute, and one of the great stately homes in Britain. Here you'll see stunning interiors, marble halls, a great library, portraits of the family by old masters, and extensive landscaped gardens that go down to the shoreline.

But don't stop there. Bute has an inner peace. Contrary to expectations, it is a pastoral island with quiet, winding country lanes that take you to the coastline, where uncrowded sandy beaches, like those at Scalpsie and Ettrick, stretch between rocky promontories.

The northern part of Bute has few roads – just the one to the Colintraive ferry and a little one from Ettrick to Glecknabae. Here rounded hills encircle Glen Moor, rising to the island's highest point 912ft (278m) on Windy Hill. Those willing to explore on foot will find the north to be a place of beauty, with sheltered, people-free coves, secret lochans and shady woods.

The middle of Bute is a haven for anglers, with several fine lakes including the most popular, Loch Fad. However, my favourite part of the island is the southern tip beyond Kilchattan Bay. Here, four parallel rocky ridges with several reedy tarns provide some of Bute's best walking. Hereabouts, the fascinating old ruins of St Blane's Church hide in a wooded, rock-fringed hollow with a fine outlook to the ocean. It's mind-stirring stuff.

The Cumbraes

Between Bute and the Ayrshire coast are two small islands, Great and Little Cumbrae. When you look across from the quayside at Largs to the low green fields of Great Cumbrae's northern end, you feel you could almost wade across – it's that near. The boat takes just ten minutes to the island's slipway, and if you miss one, it's no big deal, another will be along soon.

Great, Cumbrae may be, but it's small, and many visitors choose to leave their cars at Largs. There's a bus waiting on the other side to take you straight to Millport, which lies out of sight on the southern side of the island. Millport stretches round a sweeping bay of sandy beaches and curious rocks. This attractive town is bigger than Brodick, but smaller and much quieter than Rothesay. Like many a Hebridean fishing port, it has that rustic, lived-in look.

No ferries call on Little Cumbrae, and there's no permanent inhabitation. This haven for wildlife is generally left for divers and casual visitors with their own boats. This is a great pity, for the rugged and craggy 'wee isle' looks quite impressive, and there's the added bonus of a ruined 14th-century castle, once home to King Robert III of Scotland.

In spite of it being so close to the mainland, most visitors come to the Cumbraes for quiet enjoyment – the bigger island is ideal for cycling, has a wide variety of bird and plant-life, and some of the best beaches of the southern isles.

Geology

The study of Geology was in its infancy when in 1787 the scientist James Hutton came to Newton Point on the north coast of Arran. There he noticed the discordance between two gnarled and twisted layers of rock that could only have been caused by many separate processes over millions of years. This came to be known as 'Hutton's Unconformity', and the radical theories that followed were to be applied to rock structures throughout the whole World.

When you write about the geology of the earth, you write about the rocks you see now, and how they were formed. But, the earth's crust is continually moving – ever so slowly – with its oceans receding in one place and expanding in another. Six hundred million years ago Arran and Bute were joined to the forerunners of North America, Greenland, and the Scottish Highlands. That continent, Laurentia, lay in the Southern Hemisphere, at the edge of an ocean called Iapetus. On the other side of this ocean was the continent of Gondwana (England Europe and North Africa). As the continents came together (about 500 million years ago) and the ocean narrowed, a chain of volcanic islands was squashed against Laurentia, causing the crust to thicken and buckle. The rocks, which would form Bute and Arran, were at this time 12 miles (20km) below the surface and were heated to 600°C to form much-folded strata of quartzite, schists and slate. These rocks, known as the Dalradian, surface in the North of Bute above Loch Fad and the rounded hills on the coastal fringes of North Arran. A fine example of the folding can be seen at Imacher Point on Arran.

The Ages of Volcanoes

Goatfell and the serrated northern ridge to the west were formed some 60 million years ago, at a time when America was just beginning to separate from the northwest coast of Britain and the Atlantic Ocean was filling the gap. Fissures formed down what is now the Firth of Clyde, and the weakening continental crust along Scotland's western coastline was stretched from east to west.

Molten rock (magma) beneath the crust forced its way upward, creating huge volcanoes, at least two on Arran, and the most southerly at Ailsa Craig. The uplifted surface of the high mountainsides consisted of soft sedimentary layers, which allowed the magma to cool very slowly. The slower the magma cools, the more time crystals like quartz, feldspar and mica have to grow, and this gave Arran granite its characteristic rough grained surface.

Originally the volcanoes would have been huge cratered domes, looking rather like Mount Etna or Mount Teide. However, the softer sedimentary rocks that were uplifted by the granite intrusions were eroded by the Ice Ages and the elements to reveal the granite tors you see today.

The stretching of the land that caused the volcanoes also caused north-south cracks through which molten lava squeezed to create vertical walls of black dolerite rock, known as dykes. These can be seen in many places, including Kildonan on Arran and the Diel's Dyke on Great Cumbrae.

Earlier volcanic action, although less dramatic in the region, has left its mark. Layers of basalt lava built up and flowed westwards across what is now the south end of Bute and Little Cumbrae before coming to a halt at Corrie.

The Highland Boundary Fault

The Highland Boundary Fault is a crack in the earth's crust, running from Kintyre to Stonehaven, bisecting both Arran and Bute. Some 400 million years ago, the ancient sea was squeezed out by two land masses. To the north were the harder rocks of the Highlands, while those to the south were the sedimentary rocks of the Midland valley. In Arran, the granite mountains of the north have obscured the line of the fault. In Bute, it is more obvious, for between the wide sea bays of Rothesay and Scalpsie the channel is filled by Loch Fad and Loch Quien. There's a distinct dividing line between the rough hillsides of the north and the fertile belt of farmland to the south.

The Ice Ages

The Ice Ages brought a succession of ice sheets creeping slowly southwards from the Highlands, but with immense power. Carrying with them gigantic boulders, the ice sheets gouged out deep channels, including the Kyles of Bute and those either side of Arran. The ice scraped the softer rocks away from the surface of the granite and dolerite strata.

On Arran, glaciers formed the deep U-shaped valleys of Glen Sannox and Glen Rosa, as well as corries on the higher ground. Often the corries eroded into each other to form a serrated ridge –

a fine example of this is A' Chir on the west side of Glen Rosa. As the ice melted, it deposited glacial debris, known as a moraine, in the lower parts of the valleys. Often this debris was carried great distances, and fragments from Ailsa Craig have been found as far south as Pembrokeshire.

High Seas

Towards the end of the last Ice Age, when the ice retreated to the Poles, the level of the sea rose. At the same time the land, which had been compacted under the weight of the ice, recovered. This lead to raised shelved beaches that showed the former sea levels. As you drive round Arran's western coast road today the effect is obvious, with eroded sea cliffs overlooking coastal plains. Good examples can be found at Dougarie and Corriechravie on Arran, most of the west coast of Great Cumbrae, and Scalpsie Bay on Bute.

At the time of these high sea levels, the hill of Torr Rhigh Mor formed an island in what was the wide estuary of Machrie Water. Bute was divided into three, with tides flooding the valleys between the Scalpsie and Rothesay Bays and also Ettrick and Kames Bays.

History

The First Settlers

The Clyde Islands are known to have been inhabited from the end of the last Ice Age – around 8000BC – by Mesolithic (Middle Stone Age) tribesman. These nomadic people would probably have been summer visitors who relied on fishing and hunting for survival. They lived in caves or temporary skin huts and made small flint tools such as axes. Although archaeologists have found shell mounds beneath a Neolithic burial chamber at Glecknabae (Bute) and an agate-chipping floor with Mesolithic shaping tools near St Blane's on the same island, these early visitors left behind few signs of their existence.

Around 3500BC the farmers of the Neolithic (New Stone Age) period came here. They built their settlements, which comprised circular huts of wood or stone, on the fertile lands near the coasts and estuaries. Using more sophisticated polished stone axes they made clearances in the forests, tilled the land, and cultivated crops such as barley. Their dead were buried in collective chambered tombs built above ground and covered with earth. Examples can be seen at Torrylinn in southern Arran and Glecknabae on Bute.

The Bronze Age came late to the Western Isles – about 2000BC – as it did to the rest of Britain. Many historians believe it was introduced by the Beaker People, so named because of the ceramic beakers that were discovered in their tombs. These tribes were responsible for the building of standing stones and also stone circles, like those found at Ettrick Bay (Bute) and the extensive Machrie Moor group (Arran).

The Celts

Around 900BC the first wave of Celtic tribesmen arrived on Britain's western shores, bringing with them the cultures of the Iron Age. These were a people of artists and warriors, with the ability to manufacture swords and shields, fashioned with sophisticated tools and implements. The Celts quickly cleared forests, drained the land and planted the fields with crops. Under their dominance, the population of the isles increased significantly, but people were now richer and others wanted to rob them of their riches. Hilltop forts were built, like the one at Drumadoon on Arran. The fort, which would have been the stronghold of the island's chief, looks out to sea from the top of precipitous cliffs. As they're in ruins today, we can only estimate the height of Drumadoon's 10-feet (3m) thick walls, but they would have been a forbidding sight to the enemy. The best known of Bute's forts is at Dunagoil, perched on a promontory overlooking the southwest coast.

Though the Romans would have known the Clyde Islands well, for they regularly sailed past them to reach their bases in Dumbarton and Erskine, there are few traces of their settlement on the islands themselves. However, during their occupation of Scotland, a 2nd-century geographer known as Ptolemy prepared a map that charted the names and whereabouts of all the local tribes.

The Coming of the Scots

The next significant settlers were the Scotti tribe of Celts, who in the 4th century, led by three sons of King Erc, sailed across from the Northern Ireland kingdom of Dalriada. They conquered much of southwest Scotland, including the Clyde Islands. The youngest son, Fergus, became king of the new Scottish territories. The conquerors brought with them the Gaelic language, which was to be widely spoken in Scotland for centuries, and is still used in the more remote northern regions.

The Early Christians

Encouraged by the successive kings of Dalriada, the early Celtic monks and holy men arrived on the islands and gradually integrated the Pictish people into their religion. Bute in particular has many early Christian chapels and a monastery established by St Blane near Dunagoil. At this time the southern end of Bute would have been the most populated. The island has many more examples such as St Ninian's Chapel near the bay of the same name, St Michael's in the northwest, and Colmac at Ettrick Bay.

Viking Marauders and the Birth of Scotland

Around 800AD the Vikings started their raids on the islands and the west coast of Scotland. At first they came just to plunder. Monasteries and churches were their favoured targets, for the church had riches far beyond those of the common man. Gradually, the warriors were to settle. Eventually they conquered most of the Northern Highlands and Western Isles. The fact that the Norsemen married local girls meant that Gaelic and Norse traditions, language and heritage were merged and diluted. In centuries to come this would mean that in the islands, loyalties would be divided.

While the Vikings plundered and ruled the islands, Kenneth MacAlpine, the Scotti king was intent on uniting Dalriada and the Pictish territories of the mainland. In 843, after defeating the Picts, he formed the kingdom of Alba. By 1018, Malcolm II had finally defeated the Angles. Malcolm's grandson and successor, Duncan I, already ruled the Britons, so when he came to power in 1034, the four kingdoms of mainland Scotland were finally united. Duncan has been immortalised by William Shakespeare as the king murdered by the last Celtic king, MacBeth. MacBeth lasted 17 years until he was defeated by Duncan's son, Malcolm Canmore (Malcolm III). In the succeeding years, the new Scotland forged religious and cultural bonds with the rest of Europe, including the English and the Normans.

In the last years of the 11th century, the Norse king, Magnus Barelegs, realising his hold on the Norse territories had weakened, invaded the northern isles in an attempt to reassert his control. In 1098, the Scots and Norway signed a treaty giving the Norsemen the possession of all the islands off the west coast that could be circumnavigated by a longship with rudder set. The Scots presumed Arran and Bute would be theirs, but Magnus had other ideas. By dragging his boat across a narrow stretch of Kintyre he declared it an island, and thence set forth round Bute and Arran. It was probably Magnus who first built the castle at Rothesay.

Under Dalriada the clans owned the land and their chiefs elected the king. But when English-educated David I came to the throne in 1124, he handed out favours and land to his Anglo-Norman friends. Feudalism was born in which the kings would hand out huge parcels of land to their favoured earls, who would themselves grant land to favoured barons and knights. In turn, Normans and Saxons came to settle in the newly 'civilised' lowlands of Central Scotland.

The islanders, most of whom were part Norse and part Dalriadan, looked upon both the Scots and the Vikings as enemies. A leader, Somerled, the Thane of Argyll, who had married the daughter of Olaf, the king of Man (the northern territories) and Sudreyar (the southern isles), emerged from their ranks. Somerled sailed his galleys northwards to meet Olaf's son, Godred, in battle and gained a famous victory. He was ceded Sudreyar, which included Arran, Bute and the Cumbraes.

In 1164, Somerled was killed in battle by the troops of Scottish King, Malcolm IV after marching into the Upper Clyde at Renfrew. His troops drew back to their island retreats. The sons of Somerled were to become the Clan Donald, later the McDonalds, Lords of the Isles.

When, in 1228, Malcolm IV handed control of Rothesay and its castle to Walter FitzAlan, High Steward of Scotland, the head of the Stewart clan, it incensed the Norse, as they still legally owned the isles. The Vikings' first foray in 1228 failed, but in 1230, under the orders of King Haakon, their chiefs, Husbec and Olave, amassed troops from the islands and set sail with 80 ships to again attack the castle. After a great siege, and in spite of having boiling tar poured over them, the Vikings won the day.

Alexander III had come to the throne of Scotland and had intentions of removing the Viking threat for good. He looked first towards the lands held by the descendants of Somerled. In defiance, Ospak, son of Dugall MacSomerled, alerted King Haakon IV of Norway. Haakon and the Somerleds dispatched their ships, rounding the Mull of Kintyre before anchoring in the sheltered waters of Arran's Lamlash Bay. Alexander sent envoys to negotiate with his foe, and would have been willing to settle for Arran, Bute and the Cumbraes, but Haakon would have none of it. Some of the Viking fleet advanced to make raids on Loch Lomond. On 2nd October, 1263 a great Atlantic storm brewed up. Many of Haakon's ships were dismasted and a large supply ship had run aground off Largs. Haakon had some of his men try to rescue the supplies from the ship. But, while they were ashore Alexander's men attacked. Eventually enough Norsemen gathered on the shore to rescue the situation. The Vikings, though outnumbered, were able to return to their ships and set sail. Haakon retreated to Lamlash before returning to bury the dead. But the Vikings had lost heart in the battle: this would be their last serious raid on Scottish shores.

Struggles with the English

In the next century Scotland was embroiled in bitter battles with the English. The powerful English king, Edward I who was to be forever known as 'The Hammer of the Scots', had defeated the Welsh and declared himself King of Scotland.

William Wallace rose up against him and had a famous victory at Stirling Bridge. Wallace had many allies, including Robert the Bruce, Earl of Carrick. Bute in particular was a rendezvous for the rebellion and sheltered many of Wallaces's supporters, including Boyd of Arran and the Douglas clan. When Wallace was captured and executed in 1305, the Bruce took up the gauntlet and the following year had himself crowned as King of Scotland. But the Bruce was immediately on the run. After the defeat of Methven in 1306, he and his fleet retreated to Whiting Bay on Arran, for the MacDonalds of the Isles and their followers were far more reliable allies than some of the more treacherous Scottish barons. It is said that the Bruce watched out for the kindling of the beacon at Turnberry, which would have been the signal for his return. The signal came in 1307 and he reclaimed his crown.

In the meantime Edward I had died, leaving his less warlike son, Edward II to succeed him. As a consequence, when the Bruce did return in 1314 to defeat the English at Bannockburn, there was somewhat less resistance than would otherwise have been expected. By 1328, Edward II had been murdered and England's attentions were elsewhere. Scotland gained independence. Once again a Stewart held the islands – for a while!

Robert the Bruce's son David II ruled in troubled times. He spent eleven years of his reign as a captive of the English and was only released when a ransom was paid. In 1334, Edward Balliol took Brodick Castle and the English, now under the rule of Edward III, left Sir Adam Lisle as governor. The same year the men of Bute reacted with a spontaneous retaliation. They mounted a fierce charge on the castle. Being lightly armed, they were quickly turned back, up the slopes to a ruinous rubble fort on Barone Hill. They charged again. This time they armed themselves with the boulders of the fort and the weapons of the fallen Englishmen. When the battle was won they presented the head of the governor to the High Steward. But the victory was to turn into tragedy for the islanders. Edward sent in a vast army to lay the island waste.

The Royal Stewarts

The Stewarts' claim to the crown was a result of the marriage in 1315 between Walter, the High Steward, and Marjorie, the daughter of Robert the Bruce. They had a son, Robert, who became Robert II in 1371. Now, Rothesay was a royal castle and Bute prospered with its connections. Robert III took succession in 1390. An ineffective king by all accounts, Robert III made two notable decrees: he gave Rothesay the Royal Charter, which brought it many advantages of trade; and he made his eldest son John, the Duke of Rothesay, which was to be a hereditary title for the eldest son of the monarch. Today, Prince Charles holds the title.

On the death of Robert III in 1406, the Stewarts were confirmed as hereditary keepers of Rothesay Castle. In the years that followed Arran was made part of the sheriffdom of Bute, ruled by the sheriff's deputy, who was usually a Stewart. There seemed always to be a tension between Rothesay and Arran, or more accurately, the supporters of the Lords of the Isles and those of the Scottish Crown. Matters went from bad to worse when Robert III died leaving the conniving and ambitious Duke of Albany as regent for eighteen years. At this time the Douglas family expanded their estates, and the Lords of the Isles were left to their own devices, plotting with the enemies of Scotland. This was the scene when James I assumed power in 1424. He had the Albanys executed for their treachery, and two years later arrested forty of the Highland chiefs.

The feudal system adopted by the Scottish kings continued to alienate the Gaelic people of the islands. In 1453, James II handed lands in northwest Arran, including Lochranza Castle, to a Norman, Alexander, Lord Montgomery. This made an enemy of Ranald MacAlister, previously one of the James's supporters, and tenant of the castle and much of the land concerned. MacAlister is said to have joined forces with his former enemies, who had mounted frequent attacks on farms held by charters from the Scottish Crown. In 1455, John of the Isles and the Earl of Douglas went on the rampage, aided by monies from the Duke of York, and armed with 5,000 men and 100 galleys. After attacking Inverkip, they continued to the Cumbraes, Arran and Bute, destroying the castles at Brodick and Rothesay along the way. The Earl of Douglas later begged forgiveness from the monarch, James, and John of the Isles was forced to do likewise. In 1493, after an unsuccessful rebellion by his clansman, Alexander of Lochalsh, John, the last Lord of the Isles was forced to renounce his titles to the King James IV.

The Hamiltons and the Stewarts

Around the same time another family, the Hamiltons, came to prominence in the islands when James, Lord Hamilton married Princess Mary Stewart, Countess of Arran, daughter of James II. The alliance meant that much of Arran, including Brodick Castle, passed to the Hamiltons (see Brodick Castle, page 30). In 1503, when James IV married Margaret Tudor, daughter of Henry VII, he bestowed upon his cousin James Hamilton the title of Earl of Arran. The marriage of James IV into the Tudor dynasty meant that eventually the thrones of England and Scotland would unify – James VI of Scotland was to become James I of England. By the time of Mary Queen of Scots, the Royal Stewarts had changed the spelling of their name to Stuart.

Cromwell and the Civil War

The Civil War brought trials and tribulations to the aristocracy of both Arran and Bute. The protestant Covenantors, whose number included the Campbells and the Argylls, made a pact to support Cromwell's Parliamentarians. Brodick, under the Royalist Hamiltons, was one of the last Scottish castles to hold out against the Parliamentarians, when it fell to the Campbells in 1639. In 1646, the Campbells were being besieged in the castle by islanders loyal to the Hamiltons and King Charles I. Campbell reinforcements arrived. The Campbells then took a shocking revenge, killing, pillaging and laying the island waste. It is said that it took Arran sixty years to recover. For his support of the King, James, the first Duke of Hamilton was executed in 1649, but the family would regain their lands on Arran after the Restoration.

Like the Hamiltons, the Stewarts of Bute supported Charles I. This brought Cromwell's troops to the island. The Roundheads took Rothesay Castle and strengthened its defences, but on leaving in 1659 they destroyed the defences. In 1685, the Duke of Argyll set fire to what remained, and the castle has ever since remained empty. The Stewarts moved into the Mansion House on High Street, where they lived until the building of Mount Stuart in 1719 by the 2nd Earl of Bute.

By 1700, Scotland's economy was bankrupt and their parliament in crisis. They were forced to sign the Treaty of Union, which had them accept the Hanoverians as their monarchs. There were still Jacobite loyalties however, and many Scotsmen secretly supported James Edward Stuart, son of James II and known as the Old Pretender. The rebellion was quickly put down, and by 1719 had been snuffed out completely.

This had little effect on the isles, but the next Jacobite rebellion would. Charles Edward Stuart, Bonnie Prince Charlie, the Old Pretender's son, had been exiled in Rome but set sail for Scotland in 1745, in the belief that he could claim the throne for his father. He pushed south with an army that never exceeded 8,000 men. After victories at Perth and Prestonpans he met little resistance and made it as far south as Derby. Unfortunately for him the Duke of Devonshire had amassed a huge army. The Prince, on the advice of his generals, was forced to retreat to Scotland. After brutal defeat at Culloden, Bonnie Prince Charlie went back into exile in Rome.

The Clearances

The rebellions brought to an end the Highland way of life. The oppressive Act of Proscription in 1747 forbade the wearing of tartan and the rights of the chiefs to bear arms. The ties that bound the chiefs with their people were gone forever, and the chiefs in turn took on the feudal powers of a landlord. Those who ruled the Highland glens quickly realised that there was more money to be made from raising sheep and shooting game for sport than there was from the small rents they collected from the crofters.

Bute and Cumbrae were hardly affected, but on Arran the crofters' leases ran out, and the Hamiltons cleared the glens of Sliddery, Benlister, Kilmory, Catacol, Sannox, North Sannox, Chalmadale, along with the north coast farms of Cock and Laggan. Gradually, the glens fell silent and the cottages crumbled into the bracken and heather. A handful of the inhabitants went into small seaside cottages like the Twelve Apostles in Catacol and Hamilton Terrace on Lamlash seafront. Some were forced into the workhouses of the Central Lowlands, while others went to Canada, which was being developed as a British Colony.

New Visitors to the Isles

Luckily for the Clyde Islands, the end of the clearances coincided with the beginning of tourism. The Victorians had a lust for travel. They loved the countryside, the sea and the mountains. Transport had been revolutionised with the introduction of steam trains and steam ships. At first it was the ships that sailed all the way 'doon the Clyde' that were most popular, but later the railways would fight back in a race to be first from Glasgow to the isles. Hotels sprang up all over the Clyde Islands. Rothesay in particular grew into a sizeable holiday resort of around 10,000 inhabitants.

Great Cumbrae's claim to fame in all this hustle and bustle was a dispute between the council at Millport and the shipowners over the exorbitance of landing fees. At the start of the holiday season the ships were withdrawn, leaving the residents stranded. It took the intervention of David Lloyd George, then President of the Board of Trade, to settle the dispute.

In the early days the ships would call at all Arran's resorts, including the little fishing villages of the west coast. In the absence of proper piers the passengers would have to do the last leg of their journey in a rowing boat – but it was all part of the adventure. Brodick constructed their steamship pier in 1872, closely followed by Whiting Bay, Lamlash and Lochranza.

World War II

Bute in particular played a large role in World War II, largely due to its proximity to the Clyde. Rothesay became a Naval Base with *HMS Cyclops* acting as the depot ship for the 7th Submarine Flotilla. The Glasgow and Liverpool Salvage Company set up their headquarters at Port Bannatyne and torpedoed boats were brought here for repair. The Royal Navy also maintained a decoy village, which was lit up at night to fool the enemy into thinking it was Clydebank.

Modern Times

While tourism continued to flourish after the war, the heady Victorian days would never return. The motorcar became prominent in people's lives, and car ferries came to the islands. On Arran, the piers at Lamlash and Whiting Bay became unnecessary, because the ferries now used the shortest route, from Ardrossan to Brodick. The dance halls in Rothesay closed and, like many other seaside resorts throughout Britain, the place started to become a little dog-eared – a little too sizeable for its own good.

But now we're in the second millennium and Rothesay, with help from the Stuarts, is fighting back. Bute and Great Cumbrae have spruced themselves up for the modern car tourist and the weekend visitor, while Arran has become one of the prime island year-round destinations for the mountain walker.

And what of the Hamiltons? Well, the 12th Duke of Hamilton's only child, Lady Mary Louise, married the Marquis of Graham, who later became the 6th Duke of Montrose. On her death their properties, including Brodick Castle, were taken by the state to pay death duties. The Duke of Montrose went to what was then Rhodesia to farm and to uphold the ideas of white supremacy.

The current Lord Bute is Johnny Dumfries, an ex-Formula One racing driver who now likes to be called Johnny Bute. Significantly, he's opened up his palace, Mount Stuart to the public, perhaps the greatest single asset to the island's tourist trade.

Climate

All of the Clyde Islands are warmed by the Gulf Stream and protected from the worst of the Atlantic Gales by the mountains of Ireland. Arran particularly, with its high mountains, can be very wet at times, but even when it's raining, the sun will not be far away. Winters are mild compared with the rest of Scotland, and, with the exception of Arran's high mountains, deep snow is not a common sight.

Flora

The Clyde islands' mild climate gives first-time visitors some surprises. Palm trees grow easily in the parks and on the seafronts; crimson fuchsias flourish in the hedgerows. Even in the depths of winter, the abundant gold-yellow blooms of gorse brighten up the roadside verges and hillslopes.

Arran is wilder and more exposed than its neighbouring islands and has more of a mountain environment. Bute and Great Cumbrae are heavily cultivated, with many hectares of animal pasture and cereal fields. The grazed land is bereft of wildflowers, but the three islands as a whole have a rich diversity of flora, which I can only hint at here.

While Cumbrae prides itself on its rare orchids, Arran is famous for its ferns: over 45 different types have been found, including the Lemon-scented, the Brittle Bladder and the rare Killarney fern. Look round the bouldery banks of the burns or rocky gullies to find them. The first colours of springtime usually come with the primrose and celandine. The primroses round Loch Fad on Bute are particularly impressive. They're followed by the beautiful if common red campions and bluebells. If you're near Kames or

Lamlash and you think you've spotted cow parsley in the hedgerows, you're wrong. England's most common plant doesn't grow here: what you're seeing is sweet Cicely.

On or Near the Coast

On Arran in particular, many of the cliffs are set back from the sea leaving a raised beach between them and the shore. This provides a varied coastal habitat of woodland, acid bog, scree, pebble beach, rough grassland and salt marsh. In the grassy slopes you might find the bloody cranesbill or the wood vetch. Near the shores you will probably be able to find the blue-flowered common skullcap of the mint family, and the red berries or purple and yellow flowers of woody nightshade. I've seen the white-flowered grass of Parnassus on the grassy shoreline verges near Fairy Dell in north Arran and ragged robin on all three islands. On the rocky clifftops the incredibly hardy pink-flowered thrift grows freely as do the delicate white flowers of the sea campion. The salt marshes on the north side of Lamlash Bay are home to the sea aster, sea plantain and sea arrowgrass. On the nearby mud fringes grows the glasswort, a fleshy plant with scale like leaves that often redden at the tips. Next to it you may see the silver blue-green foliage of the annual seablite.

Woodland and Forest

Both Bute and Arran have some lovely broad-leaved woodland, perhaps the finest being on the former, along the road to Kilmichael. Here the lower hillsides and the seashore are covered by stands of oak, ash, elder, hazel, blackthorn and willow. The planted parklands of Mount Stuart I will deal with separately (see page 92).

On Arran, the Forestry Enterprise planted dense forests of conifers, mainly of imported Sitka spruce and larch. The thick canopy shuts out light, making this an inhospitable place for most plants. However, in summertime rosebay willowherb and foxglove make an appearance in the clearings to add splashes of pink to the scene. Hazel, birch and scrubby oak grow in Arran's glens, while alder and willow inhabit the marshy places around the burns. Lochranza takes its name from the rowans, which flourish by the loch shore and in Glen Chalmadale. Perhaps the most interesting trees though are to be found in Glen Diomhan near Catacol. The *sorbus arranensis* and *sorbus pseudo-fennica*, varieties of whitebeam, are unique to Arran, and are protected by English Nature.

On Hills and Mountains

Purple moor grass predominates on the uncultivated hillslopes above the forestry line. On the drier moorland plateaux of Arran and the north of Bute the soils of stone and peat are covered with a carpet of ling, supplemented by bell heather and cross-leaved heath. In the hollows and stream-heads, where the peat is waterlogged, you'll see rushes, bog myrtle, lush beds of bright green sphagnum moss, and the wispy white-flowered cotton grass. When you go higher, as on the mountain ridges of Arran, the vegetation thins to reveal the bare granite and gritty sands. Among this harsh environment you may still find something tasty – either the cloudberry or the crowberry. In the out-of-sight rock crevices and high inaccessible gullies the rare purple or the starry saxifrages grow.

While the rolling hills of northern Bute are heather and bilberry covered like those of the Highlands, the ones to the south are rockier. Sheep have eaten most of the flowers, and mowed the grass to a bowling green emerald. The odd harebell hides near the rocks and the shallow ravines are filled with bracken and aromatic juniper bushes. High up in the hills, just east of Glen Callum, is a swan-inhabited lake, Loch na Leighe. Here bogbean and yellow waterlilies grow in profusion and the island in the middle is tangled with willow.

Space Invaders

Pink Purslane, a native of Canada that has escaped from the

Glasgow Botanic Gardens has seeded itself on a hill overlooking the nearby Dunagoil Fort. More imported plants have made invasions into the islands. Near Lamlash on Arran, the 6ft (2m) high Himalayan balsam is proliferating rapidly, as is the Japanese knotweed. Like many places in Britain the rhododendron has spread from garden and park into hillside and woods. It is especially prominent around Brodick.

Fauna

On the Coast

The Scottish Islands are famous for their seals, and Arran, Bute and Cumbrae all have their colonies. They're often seen basking on the sea-smoothed rocks just off the coast. Kildonan is a likely place on Arran. Perhaps the best place on Bute is Ardscalpsie, where there are both Atlantic grey and common seals. In winter you should get a sighting of the colony in Millport Bay (Great Cumbrae), though in summer you'll have to search a bit longer. Seals are quite playful and curious creatures; they may well be eyeing you up from the water. If they become aware of your presence they will do a strange shuffle on the rocks. If you have binoculars you may be lucky enough to spot dolphins, porpoises, and basking sharks, which are quite frequent visitors to the Firth of Clyde.

An island holiday for early travellers meant feeding the thousands of hungry seagulls that flocked around the ships, and today, they're still a common sight. You may see Arctic or common tern, which visit in summer. Fulmars nest in crevices in the cliffs, especially in the south of Great Cumbrae. On Arran the peace of many upland lochs is shattered by the noise of nesting black-headed and common gulls, while on Ailsa Craig there's a thriving colony of puffins.

Great Cumbrae excels for bird life. You'll probably recognise that master fisher, the cormorant, a huge black bird that favours the shallow water near the shorelines of Millport bay and Skate

Point. Among the wading birds are the oystercatcher, a small black and white bird with a long red beak; the redshank, a speckled greyish brown bird; and the much larger curlew, with its long curved beak. Fintry Bay is a good place to see ducks and geese. One of the more showy birds is the red-breasted merganser, a black and white duck with pale brown breast, red beak and a tufted head-dress. Greylag geese, widgeons, eiders, mallards and shelduck can also be seen here. For marine life lovers a visit to the aquarium at Keppel is a must.

On Hills and Moors

Arran has golden eagles. Your best chance of spotting one is on the north coast above Lochranza and Catacol, or near the Ross road between Lamlash and Sliddery. The eagle is Britain's largest bird of prey and a majestic and graceful flier with a wingspan of up to 7ft (2m). Its 10ft (3m) nest of twigs and branches will generally be found on remote crags, or high in a Scots Pine. It was at one time hunted to near extinction, but it's now a protected species and is beginning to flourish again. The same applies to the peregrine falcon, a fearsome hawk, which scours the moors and the more secluded coastal rocks to prey on the gulls. The place you're most likely to spot a peregrine is Holy Island. Buzzards are common all over the Clyde Islands – they're easily recognised by their broad fingered wings and kitten-like mewing.

Although red deer have been sighted in Bute's northern hills, they are not present in great numbers. But Roe deer frequent several quieter parts of the island. There are two herds of wild goats: one on the northern hills and one at the southern end.

Like much of the Highlands, the high heather hills of both Arran and Bute are home to the red grouse, a noisy and plump bird, which, when disturbed, scuttles out of the undergrowth with a raucous cry of 'gobak, gobak'. Another type of grouse, the ptarmigan, lives and breeds on the hills of Arran in what is their most southerly colony. This croaking, ungainly bird has mottled grey and brown feathers that turn white during the winter months.

In Woods and Glens

In the country park at Brodick, the mature woodland is ideal for many birds and small mammals, including chiffchaff, wood warbler, goldcrest and spotted flycatcher. At dusk you may hear nightjars, for here is Scotland's largest population. Whereas in England the red squirrel is rare, you're very likely to see quite a few in the woodlands of Arran.

In the glens of Catacol, Sannox and Iorsa, red deer are prolific. In early October at the start of the rutting season, you may hear the haunting cries of the mature stags trying to ward off their rivals. Though the stags battle hard for supremacy, the fights rarely end in death. As in the Highlands, the red deer population is unsustainable on Arran, and each year between August and October the weaker animals are culled.

Britain's only poisonous snake, the adder is native to the glens of Arran. Recognised by its vee marking behind the head, the small snake is usually very timid, choosing to slink away to safety when sensing your approach. If you do see one, it will probably be basking on a rock, taking in the sun to renew its energy. Another common snakelike creature seen on Arran, and occasionally on Bute, is the slow worm. This shiny, dark brown reptile is really a legless lizard and harmless.

The Isle of Arran

Though there's a small summer ferry from the Mull of Kintyre to Lochranza, you'll probably be approaching Arran from Ardrossan, on the Ayrshire coast. Your first views from the quayside will be of Arran's distant jagged peaks, collectively known as 'The Sleeping Warrior'.

Though few secrets are given away through the haze of the Firth of Clyde, you can see that this is an island of distinction. The magnificent CalMac roll-on-roll-off ferry takes about an hour to cross the waves to the island's capital, Brodick. As the boat draws near the view polarises. Pale blue outlines become crags, fields, forests and glens. The warrior awakes from his slumber and rises to the sky as the rocky pyramid of Goatfell, the sentry who watches over Brodick Bay. A scattering of little houses and shops lines the shoreline. Gradually, your eyes will be drawn to a large red sandstone fortress among the conifers below Goatfell. This is Brodick Castle, home for centuries to the powerful Hamilton Family.

The ferry terminal appears, and about an hour after leaving the mainland you'll be driving your car down the ship's ramp and onto the island.

Brodick

Brodick is the biggest of Arran's villages, with a population of about a thousand people. Today it's a holiday town, and there are scores of B&Bs and hotels, little craft shops and cafés, all looking out to sea. You feel that Brodick holds its breath waiting for each steamer to berth, anxiously anticipating the next load of passengers to peel off in their cars and campervans.

When you reach Brodick, the first thing you notice is the spaciousness of the place. There are no multi-storey buildings to block out the sun; the houses and shops are strung out across a wide, sweeping bay, nearly all of them set well back from the road, perhaps in deference to the sea, which laps lazily against the seaweed and the sandstone rocks. And when you stand on the promenade the biggest thing you see is the ship you've just left, the magnificent *MV Caledonian Isles* with its proud black, white and red Caledonian MacBrayne livery.

There's a bus station next to the ferry terminal buildings – very handy if you've arrived on foot. The tourist information centre is in the building opposite, and next door to the petrol station. Brodick's main parking is on the seafront; so if you want a look around the village, turn right from the ferry slip road onto the Shore Road. Though it's busy in season there are always a few spare places.

Assuming you parked at the ferry end of town, the first place you'll see is the **Douglas Hotel**, a large Victorian building of local red sandstone, set back on a spacious lawn. Most of Brodick's best hotels and guesthouses are situated on hillside lanes overlooking the Shore Road. Many have pretty cottage gardens and a fine view over the bay.

If you need supplies there's a good-sized **Co-op** nearby. There's crazy golf, a putting green and cycle hire if you want to shake off the cobwebs, or there's a nice café, **Stalkers**, if you need a cup of tea or a sizzling bacon sandwich.

Pleasant greens line Shore Road in many places, and they allow an easy paced stroll along the seafront. Chances are you'll see a cormorant or two, patiently waiting on the rocks for a passing fish.

Further along the Shore Road, **James' Chocolate Shop** offers an opportunity to watch high quality chocolates and fresh cream truffles being made. Above the chemists you may notice a shop-front clock. This building, once a post office, had the island's first telephone installed.

Venturing north you'll come to the **Arran Heritage Museum**, which uses the attractive whitewashed cottage and outhouses of Rosaburn. Founded in 1976, the museum, which has an old smithy and a cottage with 19th-century furnishings, illustrates what Arran life would have been like in past centuries.

Brodick Castle

Brodick Castle cannot be seen from the road as it's set in the middle of substantial landscaped gardens and thick woodland – the entrance to it lies round the corner from the old quay at Cladach.

The castle commands a strategically important position overlooking the Clyde Estuary. Though much of what you see today is Victorian, there has been a castle of some kind here since the time of the Vikings. For many centuries Brodick Castle was one of three strongholds on Arran, the other two being Lochranza and Kildonan.

The earliest remains of the present building go back to the 13th century. Around this time records tell of the castle being garrisoned by Lord of the Isles, Angus McDonald, against the forces of King Alexander II. After the Battle of Largs in 1263 however, the islands were incorporated into mainland Scotland, and the castle handed over to the Stewarts. The next three centuries saw the castle 'destroyed' several times as it changed hands, first to the English under Edward I, then back to the Stewarts under Robert the Bruce. In 1455, it suffered under the last rebellion, by the Lords of the Isles.

The castle passed to the Hamiltons in 1503 after James, Lord Hamilton married Mary Stewart, the daughter of James IV of Scotland. They built the Round Tower, which was followed by the construction of a simple rectangular baronial-style tower. In the next century, Cromwell's Roundheads took control. They built the large battery on the east wing and extended the west wing by two bays.

Though the Hamiltons still governed the castle during the 18th century, they lived at the magnificent Hamilton Palace in Lanarkshire. During the 19th century however, the improvements to the transport system and the popularity of the isles themselves, encouraged the family back to the island. The Dukes had always enjoyed game hunting and shooting, and there was plenty of it in Arran's Highlands.

The Hamiltons had built their fortunes on coal, but two of the family's marriages were also particularly advantageous, financially. In 1810, the 10th Duke married Susan Euphemia, daughter of an eccentric millionaire, William Beckford; and in 1843 his son, the Marquis of Douglas, (later the 11th Duke) married Princess Marie of Baden, a cousin of Napoleon III. William Beckford died in 1844, leaving his wealth to the Hamiltons. About this time, building work started on the new West Wing, an elaborate Gothic-style design by architect, James Gillespie, who had also designed much of Edinburgh's New Town.

While Brodick Castle was being improved, something was happening to undermine Hamilton Palace. The expansive network of coal mineshafts that lay underneath the palace had weakened the foundations to such an extent that the whole structure was under threat of collapse. It had to be demolished. Although there was a great sale of the contents, many of the more valuable treasures, both from the Beckford and Hamilton collections, came to Brodick and can be viewed there today.

The 12th Duke of Hamilton left no male heirs and his title went to a distant cousin, who had traced his ancestry back to the 4th Duke. Brodick Castle went to his only daughter, Mary Louise Hamilton, who in 1906 married the 6th Duke of Montrose. Her love for Brodick Castle would see her taking a great interest in the gardens.

Not much is known about the early landscaping around the castle. The terracing seen to the south was done when the building was extended in 1844, while the walled flower garden beneath it goes back further, to 1710. In the 1920s the Duchess of Montrose, whose interest in exotic rhododendrons was started by her grandmother, Princess Marie, started the woodland garden. Many of the early plantings were a gift from the Muncaster Castle estate, but the Duchess's son-in-law, Major J P T Boscawen, sent a steamship full of exotic plants from the gardens of Tresco Abbey on the Islands of Scilly. Another of the Duchess's creations is the Bavarian Summerhouse built to commemorate Princess Marie.

In 1957 the Duchess died. Brodick Castle was accepted by the Treasury in lieu of death duties, and subsequently passed to the administration of the National Trust for Scotland. Since 1980 the garden has been managed as part of the Country Park in association with Cunninghame District Council.

While modern Brodick now lies at the south end of the bay, the old village was sited at Cladach on the far side of Rosaburn and huddled beneath the wooded grounds of Brodick Castle. It had two inns a row of houses known as The Street, a sawpit and a woollen mill. Ships used to call at the nearby quay, near the mouth of Cnochan Burn. Among them in the 1830s was the *Brodick*, the last sailing schooner to carry the mail from Ardrossan to the island.

The village moved when the 11th Duke of Hamilton decided to clear the castle grounds for a deer park, where he would entertain royalty from all round the world. The villagers feared the Duke's rather officious factors, the Patersons of Lamlash, and reluctantly they left their homes. Many of them were re-housed in Alma Terrace and Douglas Place.

It's said that the dukes were not that keen on the new tourism, and discouraged their tenants from accommodating the visitors. Those who did so were handed rent increases. When the Patersons quit their home, the 'Whitehouse', in 1881 it came as quite a relief to the islanders.

Corrie and Sannox

After skirting forestry plantations and coastline for several miles the road comes to Corrie, a pretty little hamlet where chocolate-box cottages look across the road to their seafront rose gardens. British Prime Minister, Herbert Asquith, called it the prettiest village in Europe.

Corrie today is strung out for over a mile of shoreline. There are a couple of interesting craft shops here – even the village store/post office has fascinating wood statues and carvings for sale (it also offers fresh percolated coffee for take-way). The **Corrie Hotel** is the heart and soul of the village during summer weekends, but those with higher things on their minds can visit the parish church, a pleasing sandstone building dating back to 1886. While we're on the subject of sandstone, take a look at the old red sandstone rocks on the Corrie seafront: 400 million years ago they were sand dunes formed in a vast tropical desert.

Corrie has two little quays, but landing passengers here used to be a hazardous business. The ships that called would stop at nearby Ferry Rock, where the adventurous journey from Ardrossan continued by rowing boat. Botanist, the Rev David Landsborough was a regular visitor to Cromla in Corrie. He introduced many exotic plants to the gardens there, which were to thrive in the island's mild climate. Among the species were palm trees, camellias, oleanders and a eucalyptus tree that has since grown to rather large proportions.

Another mile north along the road, the village of **Sannox**, whose name comes from the Norse *Sand-vik*, which means sandy bay, is dominated by the ragged rock mountains of Mullach Buidhe and Caisteal Abhail. The sandy bay is one of the island's finest – access to the best stretch is from the north side of the burn.

The **Corrie Golf Club** in Sannox is one of the most spectacular on the island, looking as it does into the jaws of Glen Sannox. Non-golfers and passers-by can also enjoy a cup of tea here. The church, which stands close to the south bank of Sannox Burn, was built in 1822 as an Independent Church, and has a twin built by the village's emigrants in Megantic County, Canada.

Before the Clearances, both Corrie and Sannox were much larger. The hillside pastures, which are now choked with bracken, were once thriving with dozens of farms and clachans (a farming hamlet consisting of several cottages and barns). By the 1830s however, the tenants were thrown out and forced to look for work elsewhere. In Sannox this meant emigrating to the mainland or the New World. However, although many Corrie residents were encouraged to do the same, there were prospects of work in the limestone and sandstone quarries. Corrie sandstone was in demand at this time and was used for the construction of the Crinan Canal and Troon Harbour. One of the victims of the Clearances was Duncan Macmillan, father of Daniel, the founder of the publishing empire and ancestor of Harold Macmillan, Conservative Prime Minister of Great Britain. Duncan had been farming with his brother-in-law on a runrig farm at the Achag above Corrie when the farm was subdivided. He left the island to live at Irvine in Ayrshire, where he worked as a coal carter.

North of the village the main motor road heads inland, but you can drive down a cul-de-sac on the right, leading past the horse-riding centre at North Sannox Farm to a pleasant picnic site on the north shores of the bay. In the forest near the hill of An Cnap are the remains of an Iron Age timber fort, while some Bronze Age standing stones are sited close to Sannox Bay.

The North End

To discover the north of the island from here you have no other option than to do so on foot, for the road to Lochranza heads inland through the wild North Glen Sannox.

The north coast and the Sannox-Lochranza road are separated by a long and wild range of hills, rough with moor grass and heather on the North Glen Sannox side, and steep and craggy down the other side to the sea. They rise to 1,457 feet (444m) at Fionn Bhealach, and are bisected by one old highway south of Torr Meadhonach (see walk page 65).

The journey round the Cock of Arran and Lochranza is one that would have been made regularly by generations of islanders before the Clearances. The tiny strip of land along the coast was much more populated until then with working farms in the Cock and Laggan areas. Coal was mined at Laggan in the 18th century: look carefully, and you'll see the remains of the old harbour. Again the Macmillan name crops up in these parts, for Malcolm, grandfather of Daniel, once farmed at the Cock.

Lochranza

The main road climbs through the wild and woolly North Glen Sannox, then plummets down the other side into the more verdant Glen Chalmadale. On the edges of Lochranza a rocky hill stands sentry to another wild glen, that of Easan Biorach, which gives glimpses of the big granite peaks. In the distance you can see Loch

Ranza, but nearer to hand is a strange modern building with copper chimneys.

It turns out to be the Arran Distillery, founded in 1996, and the only legal one on Arran for 300 years. Though it was only 5 years old at the time of writing I bought a bottle and found the malt whisky to be of fine quality, light and delicately aromatic. For lovers of good food, Harold's Restaurant, incorporated into the building, has a fine reputation.

Past the entrance to the golf course, the village proper begins and a row of whitewashed and stone built houses, including the youth hostel, stretches out to the head of the loch. It's a beautiful setting, and one as romantic as any in Scotland, with the calm blue waters framed by rowan (mountain ash) trees and bracken-mottled heather hills, complemented by the dramatic ruins of the castle. When the Vikings first sailed here, the rowans would have been a welcome sight, for they believed the trees to be sacred. For them the great ash at the centre of the Universe linked its nine worlds. Thus, they named this place Lochranza – the loch of the rowan tree river.

Lochranza was once a thriving herring fishing port with a good-sized fleet – one of the biggest in Western Scotland. Over 400 men made a living in the industry during the late 19th century. The village's castle was built sometime in the 13th century for the MacSweens of Knapdale. At that time it was little more than a hall. In 1262, King Alexander III granted it to Walter the High Steward, whose clan, the Stewarts, also held the castles at Rothesay and Brodick. Descendant, Robert, the High Steward, became the King of Scotland in 1371. James II let Lochranza to Alexander, Lord Montgomery, whose family were to occupy it for the next 250 years. It was the Montgomerys who had the towers added sometime in the 16th century. In 1705 the castle passed to the powerful Hamilton family.

If you want to view the castle's interior, you can get a key from the post office.

Continuing up the road, **The Lochranza Hotel** looks more like a large house than an inn, but it's a very friendly place where you'll meet many of the locals in an evening. Rounding the corner towards the Caledonian MacBrayne pier-head you'll come across the village's best café, the **Lochranza Tearooms**. You can sit here and watch the little car ferry go back and forth across Kilbrannan Sound to Claonaig on the Mull of Kintyre. (NB: The ferry is seasonal, running only from mid-April to mid-October.)

Catacol

A couple of miles around the corner from Lochranza lies Catacol. Huddled beneath the mountainsides at the head of Glen Catacol, the whitewashed cottages known as the Twelve Apostles were built in 1863 for the crofters evicted during the Clearances. Next door is the Catacol Bay Hotel, where Nicola and I stayed during our honeymoon. At that time (1989) the hotel was a quiet local with superb food. These days it caters for families, offering a beer garden and food children adore, such as beef burgers and chips.

Behind the village and pebble beach, Glen Catacol narrows and twists through rock-fringed heather hills. It's inviting to walkers and there are several good routes, including one to Loch Tanna.

When the northern hills of Arran are mentioned it's usually Goatfell and its satellites that come to mind. Yet there's another range to the west, culminating in Beinn Bharrain. These are smoother, rounder hills, not unlike the Red Cuillin of Skye. By the time you reach Thundergay, the glimpses of them will have you scanning the map in search of their names. There's a footpath signposted to Coire Fhionn Lochan to further entice you onto these fascinating peaks; and, if you've brought some boots, it's worth following, for this is Arran's finest corrie lake, with dark blue waters and a shoreline of white sand.

Pirnmill

Pirnmill, another ex-herring fishing village, takes its name from the pirn (bobbin) mill that was built to supply Paisley's cotton industry. The mill used wood from local forests, but closed around

1840 when the supply ran out and a modern technology superseded that manufacturing process.

The shoreline cottages you see today are mainly of the late 19th and early 20th centuries. Previously, the main settlement was at Penrioch, halfway up the hillside, but only a handful of these cottages remain. Penrioch was infamous for its illicit whisky stills and smuggling, and many stories relate to the hoodwinking of the revenue officers from Greenock, who would scour the coastline in their cutter in an effort to seize the booty.

Besides the local herring fleet, Pirnmill operated a ferry, which for many years was a rowing boat manned by two or three oarsmen. This could carry up to 20 passengers to the Mull of Kintyre. Later, an old ship's lifeboat was used. The present stone pier was built to service the Glasgow to Campbeltown steamer, which used to call daily before World War II. But the ships used on the service were both casualties of that war. *The Dalriada* struck a mine in the Thames Estuary, and the *Davaar* was sunk while on anti-invasion duties after Dunkirk. Sadly, this was about the same time the last of the herring boats were put into retirement, leaving Pirnmill as the peaceful little seaside village it is today.

Machrie, Shiskine and Blackwaterfoot

There are several hamlets along the west coast, including **Dougarie**, where an important hunting lodge at the mouth of Glen Iorsa was once owned by the Hamiltons. However it's Machrie that first catches the eye. Here the mountains of the north relent and Machrie Water flows lazily through farm pastures and low moorland.

Machrie consists of several scattered hamlets rather than one centre. The district is known more for its ancient settlements than its modern ones, for scattered across **Machrie Moor** are the remains of prehistoric communities. The most northerly one, the **Auchgallon stone circle**, looks down on the road from the pastures of Cnocan Cuallaich (hill). The six circles that surround Moss Farm date back to the Bronze Age, as do the faint remains of hut circles and field systems. Old cairns and cysts go back even further; to around 3000BC. The Machrie Moor circles can be viewed by following a waymarked footpath from the Moss Farm Gate. Choose late evening light to get the full effect of this mystical place, for the sandstone and granite blocks will glow a fiery red at sunset.

Machrie's golf club was established over a hundred years ago and has the spectacular backdrop of Kilbrannan Sound, the Mull of Kintyre and the granite hills of Beinn Bharrain and Ben Nuis. If you don't play golf you can visit the clubhouse, which is also the village's tearoom. Just south of Machrie Water's little estuary there's a fine, if small, sandy beach – a peaceful place to relax and soak up the sun.

The road climbs over the shoulder of the hill, Torr Righ Mor, where there are views across the wide valley to the church and cottages of Shiskine. The squat-towered parish church is dedicated to St Molais, who had a retreat on Holy Island. Some islanders believe that the saint was buried in the nearby Clachan Glen. The village's name comes from the Gaelic, seasgan, which means marsh. For centuries farmers have cultivated and drained this land, creating today's lush green pastures that surround Black Water. Saddell Abbey on Kintyre once administered many of these farms.

Until Victorian times, **Shiskine** used to be the main centre for the southwest of the island. Sited on the renowned engineer Thomas Telford's cross-island String Road of 1817, the village had, in the early part of the last century, a church, school, a pub, a transport depot, a library, two shops, a police station and a post office. At this time Blackwaterfoot was just known as the port of Shiskine. Today, many people associate Shiskine with a visit to the nearby Balmichael Centre, where there's a range of shops and a chance for the kids or the adult kids to be let loose on the quad bike circuits.

Blackwaterfoot grew and prospered with the increasing importance of tourism. Today it's a pleasant Cornish style village based on a small sheltered harbour and dominated by the huge Kinloch Hotel, which overlooks the seafront. Though it's much smaller than Brodick, Blackwaterfoot still offers its guests plenty to do. The Kinloch Sports Club, part of the hotel, has a swimming pool, sauna, solarium, squash courts, snooker tables and a fitness room. There's a bowling green; and the golf course, sheltered by the cliffs of Drumadoon Point, which is another of the island's scenic gems. Mountain or hybrid bicycles can be hired from the garage; this is a great way to get about Arran.

To the north of the village, there's a spectacular walk past Drumadoon Point to Kings Cave, where it is claimed that Robert the Bruce stayed while he waited for a call to return to the mainland. In reality, it is far more likely that the Bruce waited in Whiting Bay, but helpers of the king, such as the advance party of the Douglas clan, may have hidden out here before returning to their galleons. The cave is part of a fascinating system protected by four arches eroded into sandstone cliffs, and has much earlier connections to the Irishman, Fionn MacCumhail, better known as Fingal. There are fascinating cave drawings inside, and it has been suggested that this was once used as a chapel. Disappointingly, the main cave has a locked gate to keep visitors out.

Another beautiful route to the caves, and one that offers fine views over Machrie Bay, begins at a forestry car park two miles north of Blackwaterfoot. Cutting first through the forest it climbs the shoulder of Torr Righ Beag before descending to the coast.

The South Coast: Kilmory and Kildonan

The road climbs out of Blackwaterfoot, away from Drumadoon Bay, and passes along one of Arran's best examples of a raised beach. To your left are the cliffs of Creag Ban, which were once sea cliffs: to the right are the current sea cliffs, which plummet to the stony seashore.

Arran's south coast has drama and ruggedness, just like that of the north, but while the north has a Highlands feel about it, here in the south it's windswept Hebridean with a bit of Cornwall thrown in. The beaches are bouldery, with isolated whitewashed farmhouses looking out over low cliffs. There are a few houses at

Corriecravie, but the next hamlet of any importance is **Sliddery**. The name Sliddery is believed to originate from the Norse word slidor, meaning slippery, though I have seen it interpreted from Gaelic meaning field of slaughter. There is a local legend telling of Vikings being slain by the Celtic warriors.

These days Sliddery is a tiny farming hamlet in the Kilmory parish, and has lost its shoemaker, blacksmith, draper and butcher, along with its school. Hereabouts, Sliddery Water tumbles down from the hills, and through Glen Scorrodale, which has been named after the giant, Scorrie who is reputed to have lived here. Just beyond the burn, the Ross road meets the coast road, having cut across the island from Lamlash.

A short way down the road at Clachaig Farm you'll see a grassy mound. It's natural, but buried in this mound is Ossian, the poet son of Finn (Fingal).

Now the road winds and dips into the shady bowers of Lagg and Torrylinn Water. If you've built up an appetite then you're in the right place, for the large, whitewashed **Lagg Inn** lies by the river bridge. In good weather you can enjoy a superb restaurant meal, or just take a refreshing cool drink under the palm trees of the beer garden. Here, you'll be serenaded by the babbling of a burn. Built in 1791, the inn once had a distillery next door. The old kiln, where the grain was crushed and dried, is still intact near Clachaig Farm.

The **Kilmory Stores and Tearoom** lies up the hill on the other side, as does the village hall. From here it's worth taking the short waymarked walk to see the Torrylin Cairn. When archaeologist, T H Bryce, discovered the old burial ground in 1900, he found that the covering mound had been quarried and the chamber itself had been robbed of much of its stone. However, one chamber was intact and the bones of six adults, a child and a baby were found along with the skeletons of several animals, a flint scraper and a piece of dark-coloured pottery from a round-bottomed vessel.

Of rather more modern origins, Kilmory has another visitor attraction – the **Torrylinn Creamery**. From a viewing gallery, you can watch cheese being made, before tasting the product in the shop.

The road climbs higher up the ever-so-green hillsides, whose tops are ruffled with sprucewoods. A sign for South Bank Farm informs you that there are sheepdog demonstrations every Tuesday and Thursday afternoons. A short way on, there's a signpost for Kildonan, and a winding country lane descends to the shore. Now this really is Hebridean. Flaky whitewash clings, but only just, to the wind-lashed, ex-fishermen's cottages, while dark rugged rocks reach out into the surf. You're as likely to spot seals here as anywhere on Arran.

Out to sea the rocky island of **Pladda** and its lighthouse leads your eye to the equally rocky extinct volcano that is Ailsa Craig. The beach, sheltered by the fine cliffs of Bennan Head, is notable for its dolerite dykes, which jut out to sea. The dykes were formed when molten rock was squeezed through cracks in the Earth's crust.

There are two inns, both pleasantly rustic. **The Breadalbane Hotel** has a small lounge with a panoramic window so you can gaze out to sea while you eat your meals. Further east, the **Kildonan Hotel** has a very good campsite with all the facilities you need, right by the beach. Its lively bar serves traditional pub meals. If you need provisions, the Kildonan Stores and Post Office is a half-mile walk away.

Kildonan takes its name from St Donan, a 6th-century Christian monk, who arrived on these shores from Ireland along with St Columba. He started a monastic cell here, hence the 'kil' prefix. St Donan is said to have been buried next to the mill wheel on Kildonan Farm, where there are foundations of an old chapel. The neighbouring Isle of Pladda also had a cell dedicated to St Blaise.

In the history books, Kildonan is best known for its castle, one of three on the island. Today it's in poor condition with just a corner of its tower house remaining. It was once a stronghold of the powerful Stewarts. When Dean Munro visited the island in 1549 he recorded that the castle was in the hands of James Stewart,

then Sheriff of Bute. In that same year, however, James Stewart fell
out of favour with the monarchy and his lands were confiscated
and handed over to the Earl of Lennox.

Whiting Bay

The rounding of Dippen Head marks a return to Arran's east coast
– the populated side of the island. Forestry plantations still look
down from the hilltop as you descend towards Whiting Bay. Like
Brodick, the buildings of this large village are strung out along
the coast road and its wide sandy bay.

When you enter Whiting Bay from the south you first cross the
Ashdale Bridge, where Glenashdale Burn emerges from the forest
to meet the sea. Across a narrow stretch of water lies Holy Island,
though it's a bit 'round the corner' from here. To see it fully you
have to walk round the southern end of the bay to Kings Cross
Point. It's a worthwhile walk anyway, for there's history in this
secluded corner. In the 14th century, Robert the Bruce set sail from
here with his fleet to reclaim mainland Scotland. The boat-shaped
mound here is in fact a Norse burial place, where human bones,
the rivets of a Viking ship, and a coin, minted somewhere between
AD837 and 854, were discovered.

Whiting Bay prospered with the fortunes of the ships that raced
each other down the Clyde in their battle to take on board their
share of eager sightseers. In the early days the last leg of the journey
was by rowing boat, which would call at either the ferry landing
stage at Kings Cross or the jetty at Whiting Bay itself. By 1900, the
steamers could draw alongside the village's new pier. Boom time
was in the 1920s and 30s when many of the hotels and guesthouses
were built, but in 1964 this boom was over. The pier was
dismantled; no longer required by the modern car ferries, which
called instead at Brodick.

Today, Whiting Bay has plentiful accommodation, though there
are no large hotels. There's a youth hostel on the south side of the
bay for those who want cheap accommodation with no frills, and
there's also a garage, a full range of small shops, including several

craft shops and a supermarket. Of the cafés, Nicola and I liked the Coffee Pot, which had dining inside, or outside in the front garden, and served croissants, sandwiches and mouth-watering apple tart.

There's a bowling green off the Shore Road for those who like gentle exercise. For the sportsmen or women, there's a cycle hire shop by the jetty, and there's an 18-hole golf course that looks down on the village from the hillside. You can hire boats from the jetty for fishing or just pottering round the bay. If you're looking for a short walk, there's a waymarked circular forest walk from Ashdale Bridge that takes you to the Glenashdale Waterfalls, which are quite spectacular after heavy rainfall. The only problem here is that, from the official viewpoints, the falls are partially obscured by the trees.

Lamlash

The road north out of Whiting Bay cuts inland just before Kings Cross, and wanders through field and forest before entering Lamlash, the island's second biggest village. Lamlash lies on a deep bay that is sheltered by Holy Island. Benlister Burn, which flows out to the bay here, has cut a cavernous glen into the moors that surround Lamlash. While the moors rising from the glen to Ard Bheinn are bare, except for the small crusty crags that protrude from the grasses, those overlooking the bay are smothered by conifers.

In the village itself, a long, narrow green extends alongside the shoreline, giving the seafront a neat and tidy look, set off nicely by whitewashed cottages with matching grey slate roofs. The tall-towered sandstone Church of St Bride was built in 1884 by the 12th Duke of Hamilton, and has some fine stained glass windows.

Opposite the tennis courts there's a large house called **The Whitehouse**, once home to one of the island's more feared inhabitants, John Paterson Junior. Like his father before him, John was factor to the Dukes of Hamilton, and was responsible for carrying out his masters' business during the time of the Clearances. The mound on the village green has a sad past, for here on 25th April 1829 a farewell service was held for the twelve families who, during the Clearances, had been forced from their farms in Sannox. On the shores, the brig, *Caledonia*, was waiting to take them to a new life in Canada. Later, four more families would join them on another brig, the *Albion*. Descendants of these families later had a stone memorial built in front of Hamilton Terrace, which itself was built to rehouse tenants from seafront cottages the Duke had demolished.

It's quite a walk from one end of Lamlash to the other – about 1½ miles (2km) – but most of the hotels and shops are between the church and the place where the main road turns inland. There's a good campsite, the Middleton Caravan and Camping Park, near Arranton Bridge, to the south of the village. Like Whiting Bay, there are no big hotels but there are several small ones and numerous B&Bs overlooking the bay.

If you're in the mood for good food try the **Carraig Mhor Restaurant**, which is modelled on an Austrian Alpine Restaurant, both in décor and the preparation of the food. For something more basic, the Pier Head tavern does all-day bar snacks. If you're self catering, there's a Co-op supermarket, an excellent butcher of the old fashioned mode, and the Cabbage Shop, a small fresh fruit and vegetable shop.

Though the steamers call no more (the steamer pier was demolished in 1954), Lamlash lives and breathes ships and all things maritime. The position of Holy Island has made this a sheltered bay, ideal for shipping – look out into the bay and you'll sea the masts of scores of boats. It was here in 1263 that the Norse King, Haakon and his devastated fleet of galleys took refuge from the great storms following their defeat at Largs. During the First and Second World Wars Lamlash was a Naval Base. As such, it has had some rather distinguished visitors, including Winston Churchill and King George VI. The former Naval Headquarters is now the Marine Hotel, while the Arran Yacht Club has since acquired the slipway. The golf club, which in these times had associations with the Navy, is spread out over the lower slopes of the Clauchland Hills on the road to Brodick. Its lofty position gives great views over the bay, and one of the best views of Holy Island.

Holy Island

There's something enchanting about Holy Island. Even when the clouds hang low you can feel it through the silvery mist, enticing you to catch the boat, to walk towards that little whitewashed farmhouse across the water, and to climb to the top of that airy peak.

The island was for many years in private hands and 'out of bounds' to the general public, but it has now been purchased by a community of Tibetan Buddhist monks. Under the guidance of their Abbot, Lama Yeshe Losal, the monks have created a spiritual retreat for people of all faiths.

This new connection is quite fitting, for Holy Island has long links with religion, from the time when a young Celtic monk, Las, came here in the 6th century. Often holy men had the prefix 'mo', meaning 'my' added to their name; hence Las became Molas, or Molaise in the Gaelic tongue. Eventually he gave his name to the island, Eilean Molais (eilean meaning island). Through the centuries this was corrupted to Elmolaise, then Lemolash through to Lamlash, a name that was eventually taken over by the Arran village.

Molaise spent time in a cave on the island's west coast – a place well worth seeing for its Viking cave drawings. On the route to it you will see several Tibetan rock paintings. The Holy Island Project as a charity has been able to fund the planting of over 27,000 native hardwood trees, and today wild Eriskay ponies, Soay sheep and goats forage in a much-improved habitat.

Lamlash Boat Hire operates a regular small ferry from the Old Pier.

Leaving Lamlash, the road climbs past the golf course, through the regimented battalions of spruce, larch and pine, and onto the Clauchland Hills. It's worth stopping off at one of the forestry picnic sites for the walk over the hills to an Iron Age fort, **Dun Fionn**. After winding its way through heather and forestry rides, the route comes to the highest summit, where you can look over Brodick, its bay and the mountains of the north. The fort is lower and further but it's tree-free, and adds Lamlash Bay, Holy Island and the beaches of Corriegills to the view.

The Mountains and the Glens

We've toured the coast, and visited the centres of population, but now we need to travel inland; to the glens, the moors and the mountains. Though two roads, the Ross and the String, cut across the mountains and another makes a short incursion into Glen Rosa, journeys here will be on foot.

Perhaps the most spectacular scenery surrounds Glen Rosa and Glen Sannox, which are separated only by the Saddle, a high rocky col between Goatfell and Cir Mhor. Though it cuts through the highest mountains of Arran, **Glen Rosa** is a pretty glen with rowan trees and a clear bounding stream. As you enter it from Brodick the lower hillslopes are covered by forest. Goatfell, which peeps over them at the start, shyly slinks behind the fir trees. The scenery gets more exciting as the glen cuts northwards with the rockfaces of Cir Mhor and Caisteal Abhail fiercely guarding the Saddle at the head of the valley. Goatfell appears again but it's rock top seems aloof and a long way up the scaly glensides. Though once runrig farms would have existed here, now red deer are the only permanent residents. A path used by travellers for centuries climbs to the pass at the Saddle and you're truly in the midst of the mountains, looking over into heathery Glen Sannox. Cir Mhor and North Goatfell are twin towers looming above you: though Goatfell is the highest hill at 2,866 feet (874m) it's one of the easiest climbs. The hills on the east side of the glen – A'Chir, Beinn Tarsuinn and Beinn Nuis – provide the stiffest challenge, one where you need to do some serious scrambling.

If Glen Rosa is pretty, then **Glen Sannox** is dramatic and awe-inspiring. Here is a place of pinnacled granite peaks, precipitous cliffs and buttresses etched with dark gullies, plummeting heather slopes, and a no-nonsense burn that makes a straight dash for the sea – even the path from the Saddle dives over the edge into Glen Sannox like there's no tomorrow.

North Glen Sannox starts unpromisingly, with forestry covering up some of the bleakest moorland on the island. It's got a dark history too! During the Clearances, the Hamiltons left the glen's population of crofters decimated – only one farm survived. At North Sannox Bridge the road leaves the glen to its own devices, and the glen arcs southwards towards the big peaks. Though the burn is still surrounded by forestry, it has some pretty waterfalls and there's a path to see them. If you climbed higher you would enter Coire nan Ceum, a wild mountain corrie, ringed by the dark crags of Caisteal Abhail and Suidhe Fhearghas.

The mountains of northwest Arran are not as popular with walkers or climbers. Though there's crag, there's less of it; though there are cliffs, they're not as tall; and though they're above 2,000 feet (610m), they are not as majestic, nor are they big enough to be classified as Corbetts (mountains over 2,500 feet). What they do have is lochs, lochans and flowing scree slopes; they're more remote, and they're peaceful.

I've already said that Coire Fhionn Lochan with its sandy beach is the most attractive on the island, and it offers a pleasing way onto the highest of these hills, Beinn Bharrain at 2,368ft (721m). But there are long winding glens into the heartlands too. **Glen Catacol** is one of them. Seen from the storm beach at Catacol Bay, this glen is green with birch and rowan trees. Round the next bend there's a side glen called **Gleann Diomhan** where more trees crowd the burn. This is a nature reserve with a couple of species of rare whitebeam. Soon the craggy hills close in on you. You find yourself in a remote wilderness of heather marsh and crag. The river is boisterous with waterfalls and cataracts along its length. A cairn marks the col and the end of the glen. Here you look down on Loch Tanna, a large sheet of water amidst a vast tract of tussocky moor.

The longest, wildest and most remote of the glens is **Iorsa**, which begins at Dougarie and ends 8 miles (13km) away on the slopes of Carn Mor and Beinn Bhreac. Iorsa Water forms several small lochs, including Loch Iorsa, which is popular with anglers. The waters are also frequented by otters. As it eats into the mountainsides, Glen Iorsa gets more and more tussocky. Brave the tussocks by walking further down the glen and, for your efforts, you will get to see the featureless backsides of Caisteal Abhail, Beinn Tarsuinn and Beinn Nuis.

By driving along the String Road from Brodick to Shiskine and Blackwaterfoot you're almost following the **Highland Boundary Fault**, through the glens of Shurig and Machrie Water. The moorland summits to the south are seldom used by hikers, and trod by few except the grouse shooter and the forester.

Glen Cloy, which is largely afforested, allows ways into the craggy corries beneath Cnoc Dubh and Cnoc Breac, but these moors are hard going. The easiest and best of this group is Ard Bheinn, which can be tackled from the milestone near the junction between the String Road and the little lane to Machrie. Ard Bheinn has a nice mountain shape with enough crags and heather to make it attractive. It's worth the effort for the views of Goatfell and its satellites. A forest walk from Pien near Shiskine lets you into Clauchan Glen and onto the moors near Scriven, where you can detour to the remote tarn of Loch Cnoc an Loch. The loch hides in a hollow in the moors and it's a great place for birdlife. The forestry route, which was abandoned to see the burn, descends southwards over the moors to Glenree on the Ross road.

The Ross road, which links Sliddery and Lamlash, cuts through the southern hills, and reaches a height of 758ft (231m). The highest of these southern hills is **Tighvein** at 1,502ft (458m) and it's probably the easiest. Nicola and I climbed this one from Lamlash's Dyemill. Squelching through the rain-soaked forests and by the splashing torrents of Allt Leonaskey we came upon the mossy moors and Urie Loch, which eerily appeared through the mists. Tighvein is half a mile away from the loch. Today with our eyes down, we studied the mosses, rushes and moor grass rather than the beautiful views that lay beyond the clouds.

Goatfell and Broadick from the Clauchland Hills ridge (Arran)

Brodick Castle (Arran)

Glen Rosa (Arran)

St Molaise's Cave, Holy Island (Arran)

The islands of Pladda and Ailsa Craig seen from Kildonan (Arran)

Sunset over Machrie Bay (Arran)

King's Cave between Blackwaterfoot and Machrie (Arran)

Bennan Head at sunset from Kildonan (Arran)

Clearances Monument, Lamlash (Arran)

Pirnmill (Arran)

The little harbour at Corrie (Arran)

Standing stones on Machrie Moor (Arran)

St Blane's Chapel, tucked between the knolls of the south (Bute)

Lochranza Castle (Arran)

Stags on the Lochranza Golf Course (Arran)

The Twelve Apostles, Catacol Bay (Arran)

Things to See

Brodick Castle

Arran's history has always been intertwined with Brodick Castle and the Dukes of Hamilton. Built on the site of a Norse fortress, the building has been involved in wars involving many factions: the Lords of the Isles, the Vikings, the Scots and the English. Genteel as this sandstone fortress may now seem, it's no stranger to gunpowder and plot. Now in the care of the National Trust for Scotland it is open to the public for much of the year.

From the moment you go through the entrance hall the Dukes' enthusiasm for hunting is evident. On the wall hang many pictures of the hunt, while the antlered heads of 87 red deer look down on you. Upstairs you see the private rooms of the West Wing, built originally for the 11th Duke and his wife, Princess Marie of Baden. There's a collection of sketches by Thomas Gainsborough and a fine W M Turner painting of Fonthill Abbey, the home of William Beckford. Beckford was the wealthy father-in-law to the 10th Duke and a benefactor to the estate.

The Red Gallery is a narrow corridor draped with crimson curtains and many more paintings. Among them is an oil painting of Brodick Bay and Goatfell by G E Herring. The drawing room is the largest room in the castle. The plasterwork ceiling displays the heraldic history of the Hamiltons, from the marriage of Lord James Hamilton with Mary Stewart to that of the Marquis of Douglas and Clydesdale (later the 11th Duke) to Princess Marie of Baden. The library is in the 17th-century addition to the tower. Built originally for Cromwellian troops, it contains a fine 19th-century Dutch circular inlaid table and matching chairs.

After seeing the opulence of the dining room it's interesting to go downstairs, to the stone-floored kitchen where the servants prepared the great feasts for the dukes and duchesses. There's a huge Carron range with two fires and three ovens, a bread oven and a charcoal stewing-stove. Equally fascinating are the gardens. You can spend a day walking round their secret shaded corners, where you may come across the Bavarian summerhouse. The vast park and woodlands surrounding the castle are now run as a Country Park. Here you can wander for a day or go on one of the many guided walks run by the Ranger Service.

When you're in need of refreshment, try the Brodick Castle Tearoom, set in the old servants' hall (see page 71). They serve very good coffee and cakes.

Open: Castle: April 1 (or Good Friday if earlier) to 31 August and 1 September to 31 October, 1100 to 1630 (last admissions 1600). Between July 1 and August 31 the closing times are half an hour later. The reception centre/shop opens at 1000. Garden and Country Park: All year, 0930 until sunset. Tel: 01770 302202.

James' Chocolate Shop, Brodick

If you're a bit of a chocoholic you'll want to visit James' Chocolate Shop. You can look through the window at the back of the shop to the Arran Chocolate Factory where they're fashioning a wide range of luxury chocolates and fresh cream truffles.

James' Chocolate Shop, Shore Road, Brodick.
Open: 7 days a week. Tel: 01770 302873.

Arran Heritage Museum

Founded in 1976, using the 19th-century cottage of Rosaburn, the Isle of Arran Heritage Museum gives its visitors a detailed but easy to understand insight into the life of Arran in past times, with exhibits on social history, genealogy, archaeology, and geology. There's an old smithy, a harness room and a cottage that is fully furnished in the way it would have been in the 19th-century. Within the complex there's a shop, waterside gardens, a burnside picnic area, and a café that serves freshly prepared food.

Arran Heritage Museum, Rosaburn, Brodick (On the main road, north of Brodick).
Open: April to October 1030 to 1630; Tel: 01770 302636.

Arran Brewery

From a viewing gallery visitors can see the entire brewing process take place, from the beginning, when the malted barley or wheat is mixed with water, through the heating in a giant copper kettle, to the addition of the hops and the final fermentation. In the gift shop there's a sampling bar where you can try the Arran Light, Dark or Blonde beers.

Arran Brewery, Cladach, Brodick Isle of Arran KA27 8DE. (On the main road, north of Brodick). Open: April to October, 1030 to 1630. Tel: 01770 302353; Email: info@arranbrewery.com; Website: www.arranbrewery.com.

Arran Aromatics

From a viewing gallery in the shop you can watch the production of hand-made soaps, scented candles and bath and body-care products.

Arran Aromatics Visitor Centre, Home Farm, Brodick Isle of Arran KA27 8DD. Open: all year; Tel: 01770 302595; Website: www.arranaromatics.com.

Isle of Arran Distillers

The island's only legal distillers for over 300 years opened their modern distillery in 1995. The first bottling of the malt whisky began in 1999. Regular guided tours are undertaken each day. To quote the distillery's own words, 'You can stick your nose into one to smell the peat, taste our work through a little dispensing tap and see the effect of live yeast on sugar in a glass slide.' After watching a film about whisky making through the centuries, you pass through a mock smugglers' tunnel, and then take the tour of the distillery. At the end a tasting session awaits. There's also a shop, where you can buy the products along with other souvenirs of your island visit.

Isle of Arran Distillers, Lochranza, KA27 8HJ. Open: All year, but in winter call in advance for a guided tour. Tel: 01770 830264; Email: arran.distillers@btinternet.com; Website: www.arranwhisky.com.

*NB **Harold's Restaurant**, situated upstairs from the reception hall, offers some of the finest cuisine on Arran (see entry on page 72).*

Lochranza Castle

One of the island's three fortresses, Lochranza Castle's setting on a spit in the Loch is about as romantic as you can get, especially if you see it at sunset with the silhouettes of boat masts against the sky and their reflections rippling in the water. Built in the 13th century as a hall house, probably for the MacSweens of Knapdale, the castle would have taken the form of an L-shaped, two-storey fortified residence, with the master's rooms set above the domestic rooms and a tiny prison.

Though it became a royal castle when the Stewarts became kings of Scotland, Lochranza was never a royal residence. James II let the castle to Alexander, Lord Montgomery, whose family had the towers added sometime in the 16th century. In doing so they transformed the castle into a place fit for a nobleman.

A substantial section of the castle, including the northwest corner, collapsed during a violent storm of 1897, and you have to use a good deal of imagination to envisage the upper floors. However, a 1772 sketch by Francis Grose helps to set the scene.

Though it's a plain design, the enlarged three-storey tower house, with its machicolations and corbels, was furnished with watch houses, a circular turret known as a bartisan, and an overhanging embattled parapet. Inside there was much more space. The Lord would still live on the upper floors, while the domestic quarters and storage room were now down below. By this time, the Lord would require more privacy in his family's private quarters and would not reside in the large public main hall.

The fact that the tower house was built as an afterthought to the old hall house made Lochranza Castle a very unusual building. The conversion meant that the entrance, which used to face out to sea (all-important to the Norse-Celtic MacSweens), now looked back to the mountains. This tells us that the new owners were not expecting a full-scale sea invasion.

Keys for viewing are available from the post office.

Lochranza Studio Gallery

Ian Buchanan loves the islands of Scotland and is visiting each one of them using ferries and his trusty bike. His studio is in a chocolate box cottage with chocolate box cottage gardens, and has inspirational views down on the glen to Lochranza. Ian specialises in watercolours and has many paintings of Arran, in different lights and seasons. Watch the artist paint and see his work. The author did and bought two for the family dining room.

To find the gallery, take the side road, first left out of Lochranza, passing the golf course. At the next T-junction turn right and follow the cart track slightly uphill. The studio is on the right.

Tel: 01770 830651.

Machrie Moor Stone Circles

On the west side of the island, just a few miles north of Blackwaterfoot, the Machrie Moor Stone Circles are the most fascinating and mysterious of all the ancient monuments.

The six circles that surround Moss Farm date back to the Bronze Age, as do the faint reminders of hut circles and field systems. Old cairns and cysts go back even further, to around 3000BC. The Machrie Moor circles can be viewed by following a waymarked footpath from the Moss Farm Gate. There's a small roadside car park.

Torrylinn Creamery

See local Arran cheese being made by traditional hand methods in open vats. Most of the island's milk is processed here too. The cheese, made to the Dunlop recipe, is offered in mature and extra mature varieties and has won a silver medal at the British Cheese awards. The Scottish Milk Products factory can be found at Torrylinn, just east of Kilmory on the south side of the island.
Open: Monday-Friday 1000-1630 (1600 in winter). Tel: 01770 870240.

South Bank Farm Park

This working farm has red deer, Highland cattle, minority breeds of farm animals and poultry, as well as lots of pets for the children to look at. Well worth seeing are the 'One Man and his Dog'-type sheepdog demonstrations (at 1430 prompt).
Open: Sundays, Tuesdays and Thursdays, 1000-1700, from April 1 to third week in October. Tel: 01770 820221.

Eas Mor Waterfalls

The place where they say 'magical things can happen' has been a worthwhile project backed by Millenium awards. Well-drained footpaths have been created through a 'secret wooded valley' to the spectacular (after rain) waterfall, then on to a wooden interpretation centre, built from trees blown down by the storms of 1998. The centre is devoted to those who love peace and quiet. There are seats, books to read here, and pictures of the project's progress. Future dreams include a micro hydro system, on-site greenhouses and polytunnels, and a planting programme to re-instate Scotland's native broad-leaved trees.

The car park is situated above Kildonan opposite Church Brae. There's an upper car park for the disabled and elderly.
Contact: Email: easmor@talk21.com.

Things to Do
Golf

Arran has seven fine courses. While they're not championship standard courses, they are all set in the finest scenery. On Arran you can enjoy the thrill of the game, while taking in the bracing salt sea air and the views of mountain, forest, rolling green pastureland and rugged coastline. For more information on Arran's golf clubs visit the website: www.scottishgolfsouthwest.com.

Brodick Golf Club, situated right by the coast and forests of Brodick, has an imposing backdrop to most of its 18 holes, that of mighty Goat Fell. In true stress-busting fashion, the course is forgiving of those wayward drives.
Holes: 18; Length: 4,736 yards; Par: 65. Facilities: Use of clubhouse, including bar, changing room and showers. Bar snacks available. Caddy cars and buggies for hire. Tel: 01770 302349 (clubhouse).

Lamlash Golf Course, 3 miles to the south, has a splendid elevated position overlooking Lamlash Bay, Holy Island and the Firth of Clyde.
Holes: 18; Length: 4,640 yards; Par: 65. Facilities: Use of clubhouse, including changing room and showers. Bar snacks available. Clubs, caddy cars and buggies for hire. Tel: 01770 600296 (clubhouse); 01770 600196 (starter).

Whiting Bay Golf Course is hilly and looks out across the Firth of Clyde. You'll see glimpses of the island's south coast, including the little isle and lighthouse of Pladda, and ruined Kildonan castle.
Holes: 18; Length: 4,405 yards; Par: 63. Facilities: Use of clubhouse, including bar, changing room and showers. Bar snacks available. Caddy cars and electric buggies for hire. Tel: 01770 700775/700487.

Shiskine Golf Club, just above Blackwaterfoot, has an unusual 12-hole course. The non-golfing highlight of this one is the nearby small cave where Robert the Bruce is supposed to have said, 'If at first you don't succeed, try, try, try again'. I wonder if he was a golfer.

*Holes: 12; Length: 2,900 yards; Par: 42. **Facilities**: Use of changing room and showers. There is a tearoom but no bar. Caddy cars and electric buggies for hire. Tel: 01770 860226.*

Machrie Golf Course is flat and fairly easy to play. It would make an ideal venue for learners and children. There are lovely views across Kilbrannan sound to the Mull of Kintyre.

*Holes: 9; Length: 2,200 yards; Par: 33. **Facilities**: Use of changing room and showers. There is a tearoom open Easter to October for snacks. Golf clubs and trolleys for hire. Tel: 01770 850232.*

Lochranza Golf Course, on the northwest coast is set amongst glorious unspoiled countryside. Don't be surprised if you find yourself sharing the fairways with red deer.

*Holes: 18 tees to 6 double and 6 single greens; Length: 5,470 yards; Par: 70. **Facilities**: Use of changing room and showers. Clubs and trolley hire. Tel: 01770 830273; Email: golf@lochgolf.demon.co.uk*

The **Corrie Golf Club** at Sannox has nine challenging holes. Here you're looking into a fine Scottish glen ringed with rugged mountains. The course is tight with narrow approaches to the greens.

*Holes: 9; Length: 1948 yards; Par: 62 (18 holes). **Facilities**: Use of clubhouse, bar, changing room. Trolley hire available. Tel: 01770 810223.*

The **Arran Golf Pass** entitles you to a round of golf on one of six of the island's golf courses (not Corrie). Apply by telephoning the Customer Information Centre, Scottish Golf South West (Tel: 01292 678100) or Shiskine Golf Club (Tel: 01770 860226).

Celtic Links are one of several tour operators who organise golf breaks on the island and the Ayrshire mainland. Contact them at Suite 1005, Prestwick International Airport, Prestwick KA9 2PL.

Fishing
Sea Angling
The sea off Arran is a delight to fish, and you can hire a boat or go on an organised fishing trip from a few of the villages. Fish you might hope to catch include tope, rays and mackerel.

Brodick Boat and Cycle Hire
Here you can hire fishing rods, four-person fishing dinghies with

an engine and four-person rowing boats. Tackle and bait can be bought at the beach shop.

Brodick Boat and Cycle Hire, the Beach Brodick. Tel: 01770 302868 or 840255.

Holy Island Ferry and Lamlash Boat Hire

Two-hour mackerel fishing trips are arranged daily, Monday to Saturday between June and September. Rods can be provided if required.

Holy Island Ferry and Lamlash Boat Hire. Tel: 01770 60998 or 600349.

Blackrock Boat Hire, Corrie Port

Two to four-hour boat trips for sea angling and sightseeing are available on the *MV Celia M*, a fully equipped angling boat for 11 persons. Rods can be hired if required.

Blackrock Boat Hire, Corrie. Bookings and enquiries: Blackrock Guest House, Corrie. Tel: 01770 810282.

Fresh Water Fishing

Because of the mountainous terrain, the waters of Arran's rivers tend to run away very quickly. As such, they need plenty of rain to keep the levels high enough to make them fishable. The brown trout only average between four and six ounces, but there are runs of sea trout with the odd salmon from mid-July onwards. The best rivers are Sliddery, Cloy, Sannox and Kilmory Water. Sunday fishing on the rivers is prohibited.

Loch Garbad

This freshwater loch, high on the afforested hills north of Kildonan, has been stocked with large brown trout by the Arran Angling Association. There's a limit of the daily catch of two fish per rod. Not more than 15 rods per time can fish the loch and returns must be reported.

Open: 16 March to 31 October. Tel: 01770 302327.

Permits for river and loch fishing are available from the Tourist Information Centre, Brodick; Kilmory Post office Bay news, Whiting Bay and the Kildonan Hotel.

Port-na-Lochan Fishery, Kilpatrick, Blackwaterfoot

Two freshwater lochs are stocked on a daily basis with rainbow, brown and brook trout with an average weight of 2lbs (1kg). The larger loch (2 acres) is for fly fishing, while the smaller ($^3/_4$ acre) is for bait fishing. Tackle hire available with access for the disabled.

Permits can be from obtained from the Fishery Hut, Lochside Guest House (next door), the Kinloch Hotel or Bay News, Whiting Bay.

Port-na-Lochan Fishery, Kilpatrick, Blackwaterfoot. Open: daily, 0900 until dusk. Tel: 01770 860276.

Diving

There are many dive sites in the area, with wrecks off Cumbrae, Arran and the Ayrshire coast, including Bennan Head, Ailsa Craig, Ardrossan and Troon. For more information contact Anthony Wass (Tel: 01294 833724).

Boats can be chartered from Flying Eagle Charters, Largs Yacht Haven, Largs, North Ayrshire (Tel: 01294 469294).

Walking

Arran has some of the best walking in Scotland from easy strolls by the coast to serious scambles on the ridges. Here are three walks to whet the appetite:

Walk 1: Lochranza, Laggan and the Cock of Arran

Distance: 9 miles (15km); Height gain: 885 feet (270m); Time: allow 6 hours

This walk is perhaps the finest in Arran. True, it doesn't take in any tall mountains, but it does take you high enough for panoramic views of the Highlands and Islands, and it introduces you to one of the most unspoiled stretches of coastline in the country.

From the car park by the ferry terminal follow the road through the village and past the old castle. Turn left along the lane opposite to the field study centre. Where the lane turns left at Lodge Farm, leave it for a cart track signposted to the Cock and Laggan. This pleasant cart track rakes up the hillside giving elevated views of Glen Charmadale.

Beyond the last farmhouse the grassy track climbs the fellsides to join the Allt Chailean (stream). It reaches the marshy moorland col of Bearradh Tom a'Mhuide, which is marked by a pile of stones. The track degenerates into a faint path for a while before re-establishing itself on the northwestern rim of the moor. The 'green again' track rakes down beneath the dark cliffs of Creag Ghlas Laggan, and you find yourself looking across on the Firth of Clyde. Beyond the lazy blue waters the Island of Bute and the Cowal Peninsular stretch out across the skyline, leading the eye to the bigger hills of the Highlands.

The whitewashed cottage of Laggan appears on the shoreline below. The path turns sharp left and descends to it. Laggan, surely one of the most remote occupied cottages, is nearly 5 miles (8km) from the nearest navigable road, and they're rough miles at that. Electricity comes from a single wind pylon.

On reaching the cottage, watch out for the grass path through the bracken on the left. The next stretch can be rough. The path, occasionally near the shore, but sometimes higher up, clambers over boulders and forages through more thick bracken. After fording the Allt Mor at Fairy Dell the path loses itself in a jumble of rocks and care will be needed to traverse them safely. If the tide is out descend to the easier shoreline terrain. The difficulties are soon left behind and you amble across low coastal meadows. Look out for Grass of Parnassus, which is actually a white flower. Beyond the gnarled rocks of Newton Point (see Hutton's Unconformity – page 8) Lochranza comes back into view and you meet the road that will join the outgoing route at Lodge Farm.

Walk 2: Goatfell
Distance: 7 miles (11km); Height gain: 2,866 feet (874m); Time: allow 4-5 hours

As it's the highest peak on the island at 2,866ft (874m) Goatfell is a must for enthusiastic walkers. The hill itself isn't technically difficult though the other peaks facing it across Glen Rosa and Glen Sannox are.

Starting at the car park at Cladach. Follow the waymarked route opposite, passing the sawmill and craft shops. After crossing the castle's drive you enter the Forestry Enterprise's plantations. Further up, the path follows Knochan Burn continuingup the hillsides before crossing Mill Burn on a little footbridge. Beyond a tall deer fence it reaches the open mountain slopes, with Goatfell soaring above. A clear track climbs north up the slopes of Meall Breac, then left to tackle Goatfell. This last bit is steep, and over rough bouldery ground.

From the summit trig point you can see most of the island, but your eyes will be transfixed to the spectacular rock peaks on the opposite side of the glen. Many walkers return the same way as they came, which cuts out the necessity of any road walking. For a variation, there is a path from Meall Breac that descends to High Corrie where you could catch a bus back to Cladach.

Walk 3: Holy Island

Distance: 4 miles (6km); Height gain: 1,065 feet (325m); Time: 2-2¹/₂ hours

Most people do this walk clockwise, but by doing it the other way round, you tackle Mullach Mor's steep southern slopes in ascent rather than descent, which is much safer.

From the jetty, head south across shoreline pastures. The brown sheep you may see are the Soay sheep, now rare, but they're an indigenous Scottish breed. Beyond White Point the rugged sides of Mullach Beag steepen, and some sandstone cliffs rise out of the bracken. A sign shows the detour to the cave of the Celtic saint, Molaise (see page 45).

Returning to the coast path, you'll pass several boulders adorned with the ornate paintings of the Tibetan Monks, and with adjacent prayer flags. On the approach to the lighthouse the path climbs away from the shore and swings left towards the east side of the island. After a short way, turn off this path on a signposted route to Mullach Mor. The narrow path climbs steeply through heather, getting quite close to the precipitous east flanks on occasions. Beneath these slopes you can see a second lighthouse, the only one in Scotland with a square tower.

After brief respite the path gets even steeper winding its way round crags – although it's never difficult in dry conditions, you may need to use your hands on the odd occasion. A trig point marks the summit and your efforts are rewarded with a 360-degree panorama that encompasses Arran, Kintyre, Ayrshire and the Galloway hills, and the southern Munros of Arrochar and Lomond.

The path descends peaty slopes before visiting the subsidiary peak, Mullach Beag. From here it veers to the northwest before entering newly planted woods. At the far side, go through a gate and head for the whitewashed farmhouse, back to the start of the walk.

Other walks
Glenashadale Falls: an easy forest and woodland walk beginning at Whiting Bay.

Urie Lake: one of many waymarked forest trails from Dyemill near Lamlash. There are more details included in a cheap leaflet (with maps) available from the Tourist Information Centre at Brodick.

Guided ranger walks: A varied programme from Brodick Country Park.

Glen Sannox and Glen Rosa: a wonderful walk in the middle of the mountains with a high and wild col in the middle to add some spice.

Coire Fhionn Lochan: a linear walk to Arran's most beautifully sited mountain lochan.

Glen Catacol and Loch Tanna: see Arran's largest loch.

King's Cave from Torr Righ forest car park 2 miles (3km) north of Blackwaterfoot: see the legendary caves, and wonderful coastline.

Cycling
Cycling is a great way to discover Arran, and there are a number of really good routes. Perhaps the most popular is the 56-mile road around the island with its many picturesque villages en route. The climb to the pass above North Glen Sannox and Glen Chalmadale certainly gets the lungs and the legs working. You can shorten the route by turning off along the Ross or String roads.

In the south there is an 11-mile waymarked route from Lamlash to Kilmory, using forestry tracks.

Bike Hire
Brodick

Mini Golf Cycle Hire (300m from pier). Tel: 01770 302272; Brodick Cycles (opposite Village Hall). Tel: 01770 302460; Brodick Boat and Cycle Hire (on Brodick beach). Tel: 01770 302868.

Blackwaterfoot
Blackwaterfoot Garage. Tel: 01770 860277.

Whiting Bay
Whiting Bay Cycle Hire (the jetty). No land phone.

Horse Riding and Trekking
Cairnhouse Riding Centre, Blackwaterfoot is Arran's only BHS
and TRSS approved centre. They offer riding and trekking for all
grades, with hourly treks in the mornings, and afternoon hack for
experienced riders. Riding hats are provided.
Cairnhouse Riding Centre, Blackwaterfoot. Open: all year: Tel: 01770 860466.

North Sannox Pony Trekking Centre, offer one and two hour
treks for all grades, with riding hats provided.
*North Sannox Pony Trekking Centre, Sannox. Open: every day except Sunday.
Tel: 01770 810222.*

Paragliding
Arran, with its sea breezes and mild climate, is one of the best
sites in Britain for paragliders. **Flying Fever** at Kildonan can teach
you. The chief instructor, Zabdi McLean, was the Scottish
Champion, so, you learn from an expert. The firm is a member of
the British Hang Gliding and Paragliding Association. They offer
tandem flights, funday tasters, elementary pilot and pilot's courses.
*Flying Fever, No. 2 Coastguards House, Kildonan, Isle of Arran KA27 8SD.
Tel: 01770 820292; Website: www.arran.co.uk/kildonan/flyingfever.*

Tours
Bus Tours
See Getting Around (page 139).

Car Tours
Route 1: North of the Island
Distance: 40 miles (66km)
The northern route shows you the mountainous half of the island.
You get a taste on two high passes and get glimpses of Arran's
highest peaks.

   Start by taking the coast road north out of Brodick. Keep right at
the junction with the B880 String Road to pass beneath the woods

of Brodick Castle. You may see some seals at Markland Point. A turn off on the right, just beyond Sannox leads to a picturesque coastal picnic area. From Sannox the main road now climbs through the rugged North Sannox Glen before dropping down into the relative greenness of Lochranza's Glen Chalmadale. There is a lot to see in Lochranza, and it will be a while before you continue down the west coast. Beyond Catacol, the road is hemmed to the coastline by steep mountainsides, all the way down to Machrie, where flat plains bite deep into Arran's heartlands. Here you'll see the mysterious stone circles. Next comes Blackwaterfoot, a compact village with a harbour and a huge hotel. Just beyond the village turn left off the coast road and take the B880, which takes the route cross-country over a high pass, the String, before descending back towards Brodick. Turn right at the junction, following the direction to Brodick.

On route you'll see...
The Heritage Museum; Brodick Castle; Arran Distillery; Lochranza Castle; Twelve Apostles, Catacol Bay; Machrie Stones; Balmichael Visitor Centre.

Route 2: South of the Island
Distance: 31 miles (50km)
This southern route is slightly shorter and through the more gentle scenery of the south. From Brodick Pier take the road south. The route climbs through the forests of Clauchland, then drops down to Lamlash Bay, where they operate regular boat trips across the narrow stretch of water to Holy Island. After continuing through more forest you come to Whiting Bay, then round the south coast. The main road misses Kildonan, so you'll have to watch out for the signs. The road to it is narrow and winding, and occasionally you have to share it with the bus. Kildonan's castle has a lot of history, built in the 14th century for the McDonald clan, but there's not much structure these days – just a crumbling ivy-clad keep.

After passing the Breadalbane (pub) the road climbs away from the coast and rejoins the main road. This generally weaves through farmland high above the shoreline. Turn right by the War Memorial to follow the narrow Ross road, which crosses Sliddery Water before climbing to a high, afforested pass. The road descends back to Lamlash, where you turn left and retrace the coast road back to Brodick.

On route you'll see...

Holy Island; Lamlash village; Whiting Bay village; Kildonan Castle; South Bank Farm Park; Eas Mor Waterfalls, Kildonan; Torrylinn Creamery, Kilmory.

Eating Out

Brodick Area

Creelers Seafood Wine Bar and Restaurant, Cladach

Tim and Fran James, the proprietors, have their own fishing boat and they catch some of the fish you eat – so you know it's fresh! Try their oysters, or salmon that has been smoked in their own smokehouse on the island. Wash it all down with fine Chablis – or push the boat out yourselves and have champagne!

Creelers Seafood Restaurant, Smokery and Fish Shop. Open: Lunch 1200-1430; Dinner 1730-2130 (bookings preferred). Tel: 01770 302810 (restaurant).

The Wineport, Cladach

A bar bistro with a pleasant country pub atmosphere, the Wineport's menu is reasonably-priced and varied: you could choose say an Arran Cheddar, courgette and lentil roulade, with a fresh side salad, or something traditional like roast loin of lamb with garlic and rosemary. There's a fine dining restaurant that opens in the evenings only (the same menu).

Open: daily, 1100-2130 (bookings preferred). Tel: 01770 302977.

Auchrannie Country House Hotel

Here you can eat at either the luxury hotel's dining room, or the Conservatory Garden Restaurant, and choose from excellent fixed price 2-, 3- or 4-course menus.

Open: daily, 1830-2130 (bookings essential). Tel: 01770 302234.

Brodick Castle Tearoom

Set in the castle's old Servants' Hall, the Brodick Castle Tearoom serves not only morning coffee and afternoon tea with an appetising list of cakes and savouries, but also provides mouth-watering soups, 'homely' main meals and puddings. Try the delicious tomato and lentil broth or one of the naughty-but-nice fruit crumbles. When the weather is clement you can eat out on the terrace with its fine views over the gardens.

Open: daily, April 1 (or Good Friday if earlier) to 31 October, 1100 to 1700 and winter weekends. Tel: 01770 302302; Email: Brodickcastle@nts.org.uk.

Lochranza and the North
Harold's Restaurant, Isle of Arran Distillery, Lochranza

Sited upstairs from the reception hall of the island's fine modern distillery, Harold's Restaurant has panoramic views of the glen. In the daytime it's a coffee shop-cum-café, but in the evening it's a restaurant of the finest quality. The chef delights in haute cuisine and prides himself on his Cullen Skink soup.

Open: daily, 1000-1700 (coffee and home baking); Lunch 1200-1500; Dinner 1800-2200. Tel: 01770 830328.

Ingledene Hotel, Sannox

Here you can enjoy very tasty meals at reasonable prices in the bar or the conservatory of the Sannox Bay Restaurant.

Open: daily, (Bar Meals) Lunch 1230-1430; Dinner 1700-2130; (Restaurant) 1900-2100. Tel: 01770 810225.

Lighthouse Tearoom, Pirnmill

Home-cooked food a speciality. We had a huge slice of home-made coffee cake with our coffee and ate it in glorious sunshine with a view of Kilbrannan Sound and the Mull of Kintyre. Meals and snacks include huge sizzling steaks with glisteningly fresh salads; Gruyère and leek pie; macaroni cheese, and all day breakfasts.

Open: daily, Monday-Saturday, 1000 until late, Sunday: 1300-1700. Tel: 01770 850240.

The South and West Coast
Blackwaterfoot Hotel, Blackwaterfoot

The small and friendly bistro at the Blackwaterfoot Hotel is well worth visiting if you're in the area. On the menu when I was there: Fresh Sea Bass, and spinach and artichoke pie.

Open: daily, October 1900 to 2100, and winter weekends (bookings preferred). Tel: 01770 860202.

Lagg Hotel, Kilmory
Beautifully set in a wooded dell, the whitewashed Lagg Inn offers a wide range of fine bar and restaurant meals, including Crispy Coated Camembert served on a red berry coulis, Venison medallions served with braised red cabbage and port jus, Roulade of chicken with olive tapenade, Shank of Arran lamb with pommery mustard and red wine jus.
Open: daily, Lunch 1230 to 1500; Dinner 1800-2100. Tel: 01770 870255.

Breadalbane, Kildonan
Traditional bar meals are served in a dining room with a panoramic window looking out over the sea towards the isles of Pladda and Ailsa Craig.
Open: daily, Lunch 1230-1430; Dinner 1730-2100. Tel: 01770 820284.

Whiting Bay/Lamlash Area
Carraig Mhor, Lamlash
Known for its fine fresh food, which includes local seafood dishes such as lobster and squid. The menu changes daily. The owner is Austrian and the Alpine feel comes through, both in the cuisine and the ambience of the restaurant.
Open: March-October: 1800-2030 (bookings advised). Tel: 01770 600453.

Burlington Hotel, Whiting Bay
You can choose, usually from a blackboard with four choices of starter and main course. Though I haven't eaten here I have had a few recommendations for it's French-inspired cuisine and delicious soups.
Open: mid-February to December: 1900-2130 (bookings preferred). Tel: 01770 700255.

Coffee pot, Whiting Bay
This small café has tables inside, and outside on a patio. They serve delicious fresh coffee and cakes, home-made soups and salads. Try the apple tart.
Open all year: Monday-Saturday, 1000-1700 (1800, 7 days a week in July and August). Tel: 01770 700382.

Events

Arran Music Festival, Whiting Bay Village Hall

Held at Easter.
Contact: Tel: 01770 700203.

Arran Dramafest, Whiting Bay Village Hall

Held in May. Full social programme each evening following play performances.
Contact: Tel: 01770 700394.

Brodick Highland Games

A fun event for all the family. Held in August.
Contact: Tel: 01770 302290.

Isle of Arran Folk Festival

Held at various venues in June.
Contact: Tel: 01770 302623; Email: arranfolk@framei.freeserve.co.uk; Website: www.musicscotland.com/arranfolkfest.

Arran Farmers Society Show and Gymkhana

Held in August at Lamlash.
Contact: Tel: 01770 860219.

The Island of Bute

If Arran's outlines resemble a sleeping warrior, then Bute must be something sleeker and lower in the water: a sea serpent perhaps, or a basking crocodile.

Visitors to Bute usually catch the regular car ferry from Wemyss Bay (pronounced 'Weems') to Rothesay, the island's capital. That's the way Nicola and I chose to cross for the first time. Wemyss Bay sulked under heavy grey cloud. There was a fish and chip shop and a café, both closed; and a huge car park and a railway station, where in times gone by thousands of visitors would have piled off the train and onto the boat. CalMac had sneakily hidden their ticket office inside the station, and, as we had to buy a ticket we had a good look around this masterpiece of Victorian railway design. Complete with a sixty-foot clock tower and gently curving platforms, the station had a glass-covered walkway all the way down to the Prince's Pier, where the boats depart. And so we departed on the ferry, past Toward Point and its lighthouse, then onwards to Bute.

Rothesay

Rothesay was bigger than we had expected; far bigger than any place on Arran. Just like Wemyss Bay, Victorian architecture pointed to those halcyon days of mass tourism. Four- and five-storey hotels and guesthouses line the quayside, stretching all the way to Bogany Point. Behind the palm trees and colourful flowers of the beautifully set out promenade gardens there was more glazing, this time the 1920s' Winter Gardens. Old photographs in the Tourist Information Centre, now housed in the building, show that electric trams once rattled along the promenade: Rothesay is turning out to be a mini-Blackpool – no perhaps that's going too far, they don't have rock or candy floss – let's say Southport.

The **harbour** area today is smart; a credit to the town, with pristine yachts moored in the marina and a modern pier office. It

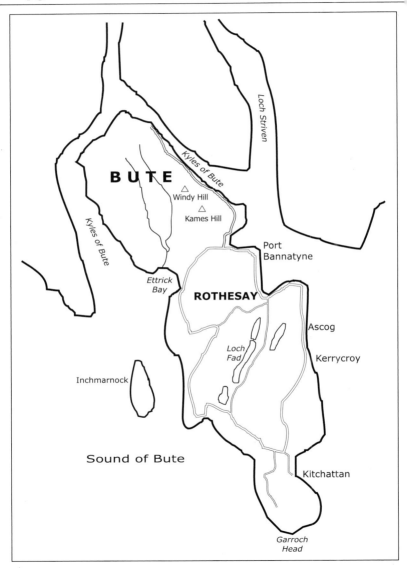

Loch Striven

Kyles of Bute

B U T E

△
Windy Hill
△
Kames Hill

Kyles of Bute

Kyles of Bute

*Ettrick
Bay*

ROTHESAY

Port
Bannatyne

Ascog

*Loch
Fad*

Kerrycroy

Inchmarnock

Kitchattan

Sound of Bute

*Garroch
Head*

was not always so. A fire in 1962 destroyed the fine Edwardian pier buildings and much of the surroundings. The tragedy couldn't have come at a worse time. Harold Macmillan's 'you've never had it so good' years had come to an end, and tourists had turned their backs on the bucket, spade and music hall holidays of Rothesay in favour of Spain's cheap sunshine and sangria packages. Many of the town's buildings had been neglected for a decade through lack of investment. In such an environment the replacement pier building was cheap and tacky, little more than a prefabricated box. But Rothesay is regenerating itself, slowly. The prefabricated box has been replaced by the current building, which borrowed from the original Edwardian design, including its pagoda-shaped roof and clock tower.

Beyond the harbour there's a big empty square. Visitors in bygone times would have seen the Bute Arms Hotel, usually the first port of call for the boisterous Glaswegian tourists. Unfortunately, the hotel had to be demolished, for its foundations had become unsafe. It's hard to picture now, but the whole area round the harbour and the promenade was reclaimed from the sea around 1839. Before this time the castle had been by the seashore.

Before venturing out of the harbour area you really should visit the **Victorian Toilets**, which were built in 1899 during Rothesay's hey-day, and restored by the Strathclyde Preservation Trust in 1994. Though the exterior may be plain – it's rather like a building from an old railway station – the interior of this gents toilet is ornate and impressive. At the entrance the ceramic-tiled floors are decorated with the crest of the Royal Burgh of Rothesay. The copper piping gleams, as do the dark green marble and glass-sided cisterns. In her book, *Temples of Convenience*, Lucida Lambton wrote that these lavatories were '… the jewel in the sanitarian's crown…'

Turning right along Victoria Street, you're in the main shopping area. Though they're quite charming, many of the cafés still seem to be stuck in a 1960s' time warp. Some of the cafés, including an ice cream parlour, are owned by the Zavaronis. One of the family,

Lena came to fame as a 16 year-old and had a string of hit records in the 1960s.

While the **Winter Garden** was noted for its music hall acts, the **Pavilion** on Argyll Street was the popular dance and concert hall of the 1930s – it's still a theatre and café with licensed entertainment. Rothesay is not renowned for having lots of high quality restaurants. On one Tuesday night in high season, Nicola and I fancied eating at **Fowlers**, a bustling waterside bistro at the back of the Winter Garden. So, dressed to the nines, we trotted along the promenade only to find that Fowlers wasn't bustling at all. On reading the notices we saw that it closes on Monday evenings and Tuesdays. Instead, we ended up in the **Jade Garden**, a little Chinese Restaurant that came complete with goldfish in a tank and an all-Scottish staff quota (though they probably had a Chinese chef chained to his wok somewhere in the kitchens). The food was delicious and the wine, reasonable (a pleasant bottle of Minervois cost £8). We were later to stay at the **Ardyne St Ebba Hotel** on Mount Stuart Road and used their restaurant. Here, an excellent Pouilly Fumé complemented the garlic chicken supreme to perfection. **Fowlers**? It was worth waiting for, but we had to wait until our next trip in late September.

I've mentioned the splendid Winter Garden building, but particularly impressive are the park-like gardens round it. Beneath the swaying palm trees are colourful roses and beautifully cared-for beds of annuals. There's a putting green with a statue of 19th-century Governor of Bute, Alexander Bannatyne Stewart, watching out for any rogue shots or transgressions on the green.

Facing Rothesay Castle are the imposing castellated **County Buildings and Prison** of 1832. On the other side, the **Bute Museum** (see page 105), built in 1927 by the 4th Marquis of Bute for the Buteshire Natural History Society, offers an insight into the life and times of the island, with some fascinating information about the island's Naval history.

The history of **Battery Place** and how it came to be so named goes back to the Napoleonic Wars. When the French General's

Rothesay Castle

By turning up Tower Street you'll come to the old part of town, where the 14th-century Rothesay Castle is perched on a grassy mound, surrounded by a deep moat.

Although the earliest history is unclear, there has been a castle at Rothesay since the times of the Vikings, when it would have been on the shoreline, looking out to sea. It is known that the Stewarts took control of the castle in 1164, when King Malcolm IV handed it to Walter FitzAlan, the High Steward of Scotland after defeating Somerled at Renfrew.

Though the castle was never a great fortress – its walls were too thin to resist canon and gunpowder – it had a traumatic and violent lifespan, being flattened on several occasions. In 1230, it was sacked by the Vikings under King Haakon before being recaptured by the Scots. It passed into English hands in the time of Edward I. Perhaps one of the bloodiest and most famous battles was inspired by Robert the Bruce's victory at Dunoon, for the islanders, armed with stones from an old fort on Barone Hill, stormed the castle and murdered its English governor, Sir Adam Lisle. This brought the wrath of the English upon Bute. It was flattened and laid waste for 60 years.

Rothesay became a royal castle, when Walter the High Steward's son became King Robert II of Scotland. The connections were good for Rothesay and the castle became a power base. On the death of Robert III in 1406, the Stewarts were confirmed as hereditary keepers of the castle.

The dynasty was loyal to King Charles I, but were to pay for it dearly. When Cromwell's troops arrived on Bute they garrisoned the castle and reinforced its defences. However, on leaving, the roundheads destroyed those defences. The castle was still habitable though, until 1685, when the Argyll Highlanders, under the orders of the 9th Duke of Argyll, burnt it down. The castle has been empty ever since.

The Stewarts moved into the Old Mansion House on the High Street, which had been intended for a local businessman. The four-storey whitewashed building is still used by the Bute Estates Office. The castle has been tidied up and partially restored by the 2nd and 3rd Marquesses of Bute.

threat was at its greatest Rothesay formed a volunteer association to defend the town. They mounted a battery of guns on this street facing out to sea. The captain of the battery had Glenburn House built for himself.

The area of town between Battery Place and Craigmore Pier was the more affluent one and today several well-appointed hotels still offer plentiful accommodation. The huge **Glenburn Hotel** was built in 1890 as a Hydropathic Hotel, to pander to the health-conscious, wealthy Victorian traveller.

Skipper Woods, named on the map as Bogany Wood, cloaks the sides of Canada Hill, above the Battery Place rooftops. It's a fine place for easy walks, but has a melancholy past, for the name **Canada Hill** comes from the times of the Clearances when displaced families would come up here to have one last look at their island before embarking on their long journey to their new country and a new life. Nowadays there's a golf course on top with those same lovely views over the Firth of Clyde. Next door there are two campsites and a horse-riding centre. If you like steps, there's another way up Canada Hill from the town centre. The Serpentine consists of a narrow road zigzagging up and up a narrow strip of grass-covered parkland separating rows of opulent Victorian houses. Linking each zag is a wide, steep flight of stone-built steps. I do not recommend driving your car up this road to get to the top of the hill: take Eastlands Road past the Ardencraig Gardens and the Rothesay Riding Centre instead.

Doon the Watter

The fortunes of Bute, and Rothesay have been inextricably linked to the sea and ships; from the Viking marauders, to freedom and the Battle of Largs, and more recently, to the famous steamers that plied their trade 'doon the watters' of the Clyde.

In the early years of the 19th century, the ships sailed exclusively from Glasgow's Broomielaw Docks, but soon there were over seventy steamer piers on the Clyde, and Rothesay had a hundred calls a day from around forty ships. Competition was rife and the rules were few. Races and dirty tricks were commonplace, making travel on a Clyde steamer an unforgettable experience.

Captain Price, skipper of the *Ruby*, was one of the more colourful characters of the day and had been involved in many 'incidents'. In one famous race between the *Ruby* and the *Rothesay Castle*, skippered by Captain Brown, the *Rothesay Castle* won in record time. Unfortunately, this brought the matter to the attention of the courts and both skippers were fined for reckless navigation.

The occurrences of collisions, the omission of scheduled pier stops to get to the next stage first, and the early lifting of gangplanks so that passengers couldn't embark, were getting all to common for the editor of the *Glasgow Herald*, who wrote: 'What right has this man Price to entrap people into his vessel for a safe summer-day sail and then subject them to terror of a violent death by explosion or collision?'

By the end of the 19th century, the rail-steam packages had entered the market with railway piers being constructed at Gourock, Greenock and Wemyss Bay. They competed for trade with the all steamship packages from Glasgow. The races continued. There were some epic encounters between the *Columba* and the *Lord of the Isles* in their scheduled 10 o'clock sailing for Rothesay. These would attract crowds along the promenades.

For all the misdemeanours, there have not been many serious accidents over the years. In 1890, the *Scotia* and the *Duchess of Hamilton* collided; in 1907 the *Kintyre* was sunk after colliding with a steamer off the Skelmorlie coast; in 1935 the *Duchess of Rothesay* sank, and a year later the *Duchess of Fife* ran aground.

In 2002, only two services run to Bute: one between Wemyss Bay and Rothesay, and the other between Colintraive and Rhubodach. However, there's still one romantic reminder of those days of steam: the restored paddle steamer, *Waverley*, still berths regularly at Rothesay for pleasure trips to the mainland lochs and the islands. It's a wonderful way to see the area!

I've written so far only about Rothesay, and, although most of the population, entertainment and the hotels are here, Bute has so much more to offer. We are now about to explore the quiet and subtle side of the island; the island of sandy beaches, rocky coves, ancient oakwoods, heather hills and secret tarns.

Port Bannatyne and Kames

Besides Skeoch Woods there's no real countryside between Rothesay and Port Bannatyne: just a sign to say you've left one and entered the other. Port Bannatyne's a ribbon development with a high (main) road and a low promenade. The coastline curves left away from Rothesay Bay into the stony Kames Bay. It's pleasant enough, but at first glance, there's not much to persuade you to halt your journey for too long unless you're looking for a berth for your yacht in the marina.

Like Rothesay, **Port Bannatyne** has strong links with the sea, from the times when the port was busy with herring boats and puffers to the time when McIntyre's shipbuilding yard was in full swing. The village was until the mid-19th century known Kamesburgh, but the Marquis of Bute changed it in honour of the Bannatyne family of Kames Castle. The Bannatynes moved from their Ayrshire seat in the 15th century, and were granted the charter of Kames after sending four sons to the ill-fated Battle of Flodden.

Beyond Port Bannatyne the road splits. One road continues round the bay to the ferry at Rhubodach: the other heads eastwards towards Ettrick Bay. **Kames Castle**, which sadly isn't open to the public, stands in fields close to the junction. The 14th-century tower house, now surrounded by farm buildings, was once encircled by a moat, though there's not much trace of that now.

Ettrick Bay and the North of the Island

Beyond the castle the road continues through pastures sheltered by Bute's highest hills. Halfway to Ettrick there's a roofless church, once dedicated to St Colmac. In fields on the opposite side are the even older ruins of a Bronze Age stone circle, where some gaunt looking wind-warped trees add drama to the scene. The road splits

Bute's Electric Trams

It was 1879 and Bute was in the boom years. Visitors arrived on the island in droves, and a new company had formed with big ideas. The island had very little in the way of public transport and the men who formed the Rothesay Tramways Company started work on a line that would operate from Rothesay's Guildford Square round the bay to Port Bannatyne. After dealing with the inevitable planning protests the line opened in 1882, with horse-drawn trams timetabled to run every 15 minutes between the resorts – the journey time was set at half an hour.

In a study of 1969, Bute's County Librarian, Allan Leach described how the drivers would try to beat the journey time in order to extend their refreshment breaks. He mused that the horses also had become wise to the situation when he wrote, 'some horses knew this as well as their drivers, and one in particular had the reputation that when the other end of the journey represented time to enjoy a nosebag he would set off from Rothesay as though the furies were after him...'

In those pioneering days delays were caused by the lack of passing points in the single track. Passengers complained about the lack of comfort in the original open-topped tramcars. Within a year the tramcars had been rebuilt and supplemented by new closed-roof cars, and the delays were made negligible by the addition of loop lines. Though the company had received stiff competition from horse-drawn buses the tramway was now a success story. The next stage was electrification.

By 1902 the line was electrified and trams were speeding along the coast at up to 20mph. The public objected to these 'dangerous speeds' and their complaints were reinforced by a fatal accident. Undaunted, the company went ahead in 1905 with the next stage, a line from Port Bannatyne to Ettrick Bay. Unusually, the track wasn't routed along the road, but on sleepers laid across the meadows. Almost certainly this was the most scenic tramway in the whole of Britain. To popularise the route the company arranged musical concerts, dances, fairs, and sports days. Ettrick's idyllic sandy bay became a busy little place.

By the mid 1920s, motorbuses had become a serious threat. The tram company had itself bought some buses and were soon using them exclusively during the winter months. The inevitable happened on the 30 September 1936 when the last tram left Guildford Square for Port Bannatyne.

again. We'll take the right fork for now, a cul-de-sac, and head for the north side of Ettrick Bay.

Ettrick Bay is a fine white sandy beach, about a mile long and framed by farm pastures, hedgerows and low hills. There's a small tarred car park and a snack bar, the last reminders of an era when the tramcars came up the valley from Rothesay.

To the north of Ettrick Bay a narrow lane traces the coastline to **Glecknabae**, an area known for its Neolithic burial chambers and early settlements. The road ends at a small car park. Nearby Glecknabae Cairn dates back to 3000BC, but when archaeologists excavated further they found that beneath the chamber were remnants of a kitchen midden containing the shells of oysters, whelks and limpets. The find showed this to be among the earliest settlements on Bute: one likely to have been left by the Mesolithic hunters who inhabited the land after the last Ice Age.

Beyond the road, an unsurfaced cart track heads north parallel to shoreline woods. There's another Neolithic long cairn, Cairn Ban, above South Lenihuline Woods. **Lenihuline** means halfpenny holly and indicates that the farm once sited here must have had a rental value of a halfpenny – the holly trees still exist here.

St Michael's Grave is also Neolithic, but has nothing to do with the saint of that name. Lying in the field before Kilmichael Cottage, the collapsed chamber looks out from a fine vantage point across the Kyles of Bute. Down near the shoreline are the ruins of an old ferry house, which operated from the late 17th century across the Kyles of Bute to Kames (across the Kyle on Cowal). In 1700, the ferryman, William Blair, was one of the victims of a clamp down against Sabbath Breakers. He was ordered under penalty not to row passengers on Sunday unless 'they can evidence the same to be upon urgent necessitie'. You can still just about make out the foundations of the Blair's cottage just, and also the adjoining waiting room/inn, which was known as the Bottle and Glass.

Further north perched on a grassy knoll, **Kilmichael Chapel** has been dedicated to the 6th-century St Maccaile. The ruin contains the stone altar and aumbrey (a recess for storing church vessels). Historians believe the upper walls are too haphazardly built to be part of the original Celtic chapel. On the south side the chapel walls have been built over the remains of a Bronze Age cyst, which is over a thousand years older.

Adventurers who don't need waymarked paths will be in their element here, though these are sensitive areas for wildlife conservation. Little craggy coastal hillocks, and deserted bays of sand and cobbles stretch out to the very northern tip at Buttock Hill – how strange that Bute's buttock should be at the top! Views across the narrow Kyles to the wooded hills above Kames and Tighnabruaich are stunning.

The **Maids of Bute** are two painted rocks, which are best seen from a boat. According to Neil Munro in his fictional *Tales of Para Handy*, the first person to paint the rocks was Peter McFarlane, alias Para Handy who said of them, 'The North end o' Bute iss a bleak, wild, lonely place, but when I wass done pentin the Maids it looked like a large population.'

The northeast side of Bute has been cloaked with conifers though there are remnants of the old birch, oak and alder woods nearer the shores. The long distance footpath, the **West Island Way** begins from near the ferry at Rhubodach before climbing onto these hills but the observant will notice Bull Loch, a patch of blue on the map. The lochan is wild, lonely and romantic, its rushy shoreline surrounded by pale moor grass wetlands and the odd scrub birch. Rocks on the heather hills make an ideal picnic spot, and you can sit watching out for the wildlife – a grouse, a kestrel, or a buzzard.

The West Island Way descends to Glen More's farm pastures. It's from hereabouts that you should tackle Bute's highest peak,

Windy Hill, 911ft (278m). Most walkers climbing this hill park their cars at Ettrick Bay's northern car park.

Inchmarnock and the Western Bays

The A844 goes to the quieter south side of Ettrick Bay before cutting inland of Watch Hill. Like many of the roads on Bute, if you don't watch for the signposts, you'll end up back at Rothesay. **St Ninian's Bay** is well worth seeing. To get there you leave the main road for one signed to Straad, now a handful of cottages just short of the beach. Until the start of the 20th century, Straad was a thriving community, based on a prosperous fleet of herring boats. It had two inns, a schoolhouse, a joiner, two cobblers, a blacksmith, a cooper and a miller. Most of the villagers kept donkeys, which they used to ferry the fish to and from the boats and a kippering shed on the far side of the bay. Those donkeys in need of a rest were sometimes sent to Inchmarnock for summer grazing. Once, it was reported that four of the donkeys swam back across the dangerous waters of the firth.

St Ninian's Bay is completely different to that of Ettrick. It is deeply inset and spacious, and bisected by a narrow grassy isthmus with a whitewashed crofters cottage on the end. Some of the sand has been substituted by seaweed and cobbles, crusted with thousands of muscles. On a clear day, as you contour round from the east to the west side of the bay, you can see the island of Inchmarnock backed up by the imposing craggy peaks of Arran's Sleeping Warrior. Some standing stones lie in the field to the right

Beyond the croft you come to the ruins of **St Ninian's Chapel**, which were unearthed in 1952-4 by W Glen Aitken. St Ninian was a Celtic monk who, after visiting Rome, set up a chapel on the Isle of Whithorn. Today, the surrounding grassland is enveloping what remains of the chapel's rubble walls. Archaeologists have dated the chapel back to either the 6th or 7th century – a long time after the death of St Ninian. It therefore seems likely that some of the saint's disciples were the founders. The chapel was raided and destroyed by Vikings during the 8th century. Next door to the chapel are the ruins of the old kippering shed where herrings were smoked.

Inchmarnock

Inchmarnock is small, just 2$^1/_2$ miles by $^1/_2$ mile; it's fertile, with its lush green fields and hedgerows; and it's just a mile offshore from the west of Bute. However, at the time of writing, it's uninhabited, and left for the wildlife.

Inchmarnock was named after St Marnoc, who came here sometime in the 7th century to set up a monastery, which was probably attached to the Cistercian monastery of Saddel on Kintyre. Some of the remains are still evident today.

In 1961, archaeologists discovered a group of three burial cysts at the north end of the island. Further excavation revealed a young woman's skeleton, a flint knife, and, by her side, 135 scattered beads from a necklace. The Inchmarnock Necklace has been restrung and is now displayed in Bute's Natural History Museum. It is estimated to be 3,500 years old.

There were three farms on the island, namely, North, Mid and South Park and during the 19th and early 20th centuries the population remained between 15 and 20 people. Like many of the Scottish Isles, Inchmarnock was notorious for its smugglers. Life would have been hard, for the island was often cut off from Bute and the mainland – currents in the channel between Inchmarnock and Bute are notoriously dangerous in poor weather conditions.

In 1943, the British Government evacuated the island so that it could use it as a long-range gun target. Mysteriously, the farm of South Park disappeared from the map after being burned down before the army left.

Now Inchmarnock is known more for its seabirds and flowers than its people. Skuas, terns, fulmars and gulls thrive here, while buzzards and peregrine falcons scour the fields for prey. The foreshore, woods and meadows are rich with red campion, scarlet

Robert Thom's Cuts

It was 1813. Rothesay's cotton mills were vital to the town's prosperity, employing 700 cotton workers and 200 weavers. But Rothesay's cotton mill was failing, and almost into the bankruptcy courts. Arch Moore, the factor, had written a gloomy prognosis to the master, Lord Bute. 'The Cotton Mills I dare say will not sell at all at present unless some favourable change takes place on the Continent.'

But sold they were, to a firm called Kelly and Thom. Robert Thom, a water engineer from Greenock, realised that to flourish the mills would need to expand, and that expansion would require a reliable and independent water supply. Over the next decade he planned and constructed a series of water lades, aqueducts and bridges known as Thom's Cuts – nearly 7 miles in all – conveying water from the surrounding hillsides and lakes to the Kirk Dam and Loch Fad. The Birgidale Cut drained the west side of the Central Moors, while the Quien Cut, the easiest to see, followed the line of the main road above Scalpsie Bay. Another, starting at Drumreoch, wandered round Scoulag Moor above Mount Stuart before descending into Loch Fad by Barnauld. This has now been diverted to flow into Loch Ascog.

Unfortunately Thom's cut on Scoulag Moor landed him in trouble, for it cut off the supply to the Marquess of Bute's Mount Stuart! The scheme on the whole, however, was successful, and the mills expanded rapidly: by the 1820s they were employing 1,000, and even more in 1840 – one mill alone employed 350 at this time. Unfortunately, in the last years of the century Bute's cotton industry dwindled into insignificance, mainly due to transport and communications problems. Though some are obscured by agricultural workings, Thom's cuts still survive, and many of the aqueducts and bridges can still be seen. Discovering these masterworks of engineering can involve you in a fascinating exercise of detective work, but the map in the Natural History Museum at Rothesay can help you.

pimpernel, thrift and primroses, as well as the rarer oyster flower. Needless to say, the seals like the new found peace, too.

Loch Fad and the Highland Boundary Fault

Beyond St Ninian's Bay and Inchmarnock, the road runs beneath and alongside the range of hills that form the northern sides of a lake-filled central valley. As you round the most southerly summit, Tarmore Hill, you find yourself looking down on **Scalpsie Bay**. Watch out for a small car park in an old quarry on the left: it's easy to miss. From here there are two very short but worthwhile signposted walks. The first goes to Tarmore Hill and offers memorable panoramas of Southern Bute and Inchmarnock. You can also see across Loch Quien to the valley I've just mentioned. Geologically, the valley is very important, for it marks the course of the Highland Boundary Fault, a crack in the Earth's crust that runs from Kintyre to Stonehaven. Here on Bute it's a distinct dividing line between the rough hillsides you're standing on, and the fertile belt of farmland you can see to the south.

The other walk descends across a field to a seal viewing point in the trees. There's also a wonderful view of Scalpsie Bay's yawning sands, framed by the receding bays of Gallachan, Stravanan and Dunagoil. Beyond a beautifully sited picnic table, a devious little path scrambles down to the shore where you can get an even closer look at the seals. The main car park for visiting Scalpsie Bay's beach lies a mile further along the road, opposite Loch Quien, and its just a short walk across fields to get to the sands.

Loch Quien is one of three lakes on the Highland Boundary fault, the others being **Loch Fad** and the **Kirk Dam Reservoir**. It has two of the island's three crannogs (bronze-age dwellings built on artificial log islands – the other is on nearby Loch Ddu). The causeway that led to them is now underwater. At nearly 2 miles (3km) long, Loch Fad is the largest of Bute's freshwater lochs (in Gaelic fada means long). In the 18th century, it supplied the water for Rothesay's linen industry.

Bute's rushy central lochs have been designated a Site of Special Scientific Interest to protect their status as a refuge for wildfowl and other birds. Teal, moorhen, grebe, widgeon, mute swans and coot are all here. Around the lochs and in the woods you'll see goldfinches, yellow wagtails, yellowhammers, woodpeckers and cuckoos. There's a bird hide overlooking the Kirk Dam.

Loch Fad's most famous for fish, and though the fishing is controlled, the waters are well stocked with both rainbow and brown trout – there's said to be a huge pike in the depths. Anglers come from all over the World, either to fish from the banks, or from one of the many hire-boats.

Kingarth, Kilchattan Bay and the South Coast

The A-road continues through fields full of cows and corn; past farmhouse after farmhouse. There's the quietest golf course I've ever seen, right by the sands of Stravannan Bay; then you come into Kingarth, where a few houses and farms cluster around the whitewashed inn. The Kingarth Hotel is popular, and the owners are proud that it is Bute's only country pub. If it's the weekend in season you may have to book for a bar meal here, though it's worth it, especially in the Garden Restaurant, where the emphasis is on game and fresh local produce.

In medieval times, Kingarth was the most populated part of Bute, and its inhabitants were almost independent from the rest of the island, being descendants of the tenants who had been granted a charter and protections by James IV in 1506. Unlike those of the rest of the western isles, most of Kingarth's medieval farms exist today, as do many of the families that farmed them. The McCaws of Garrochty, for instance, can trace their ancestry back to the times of Alexander II.

In the 19th century, **Kingarth** was best known for its tile works, which opened in 1849 and utilised the local red sandstone. At its peak, 20 men churned out about 1.25 million tiles and bricks each year. Many were used locally on Bute, but the works also exported them on a fleet of smacks based at Kilchattan. The factory closed its door for the last time in 1915 and Kingarth returned to farming.

It's just a mile from Kingarth to the sea, but in that mile the island's character changes totally. First, you come to the seashore; an empty bay with dancing rushes and wide pink sands looking out across the water to Great Cumbrae. Then you turn right into Kilchattan, where a row of terraced cottages and a hotel line the seafront, with their backyards built into the steep wooded hillsides behind. This village is small, but its houses seem to have been plucked from an urban street.

Kilchattan is dedicated to the 6th century monk, St Catan, a disciple of the Irish Church of Patrick. Catan came here in his retirement. It is often written that he was the nephew of St Blane.

Among the hills that shade the village from the evening sun, the highest is Suidhe Chatain, which means St Catan's seat. It's a steep compact little peak 515ft (157m) high with a magnificent view of both sides of the islands, including the fascinating rock knolls of the south, the islands of Cumbrae and the blue waters of the Firth of Clyde. There's a marked path to the summit from the back of the village, or you can include it in a coastal traverse of Glencallum Bay (see page 114).

Until the mid-19th century, Kilchattan had been a sleepy little fishing village with about 50 cottages. But the tileworks of Kingarth and tourism brought with it more people and prosperity. In 1880, a pier was built and the ships began to call. At one time Kilchattan had its own regular steamship service from Wemyss Bay, Fairlie and Millport, with excursion ships also berthing. A hotel was built, and industrialists moved into large villas overlooking the bay. But the steamships stopped coming, replaced by the car ferry services that berthed at Rothesay and Rhubodach. Kilchattan returned to the sleepy little village it once was.

Kilchattan and its road end at a five-bar gate. Beyond it, there's just craggy hills, rocky coastal bluffs and relics of ancient history. It's the most romantic area of the island. The prominent Hawk's Nib is an outcrop of columnar sandstone containing the embedded fossils of Ganoid fishes that are believed to be over 200 million years old. Over the next bluff you'll be looking down on **Glencallum Bay**, which is as good as Bute's seaboard gets. The bay is deeply indented, with a shingle beach, sheltered by two high and rocky promontories. The eastern promontory, Rhub'an

Mount Stuart

When the Duke of Argyll set fire to and destroyed Rothesay Castle he left the Stuarts with no proper place to go. The Old Mansion House in Rothesay that they had acquired was comfortable, but for Scotland's foremost family, it wasn't grand enough.

The name Mount Stuart first appears when Sir James Stuart received the title, 1st Earl of Bute, and Lord Mount Stuart in 1703, but the first plans for the house there were drawn up in 1716 by Alexander McGill for the 2nd Earl. Though there were many delays in the building of the house, the Earl persevered with his plans for the extensive gardens, ordering seeds from all over the World through William Millar, the seedsman at Holyrood Palace. He had thousands of trees planted, including 500 beeches, 1,000 yew, 4,000 thorns, with pear, apple, cherry and plum trees making up the numbers.

By 1719, the house was complete and the gardens were beginning to flourish. This first house was of simpler design than the one you see today, with three storeys, a hipped roof, Palladian wings, and with staircases housed into turrets at each end.

Unfortunately, the 2nd Earl wasn't able to enjoy the house for long: he died only a few months after its completion. His son, John Stuart, was still a small boy at this time, but had learned to love both the island and the house. The 3rd Earl would develop the house and grounds still further, though through his commitments, he would spend a good deal of time away from the place. In a rise to fame the Earl would become first tutor to George III, then a Knight of the Garter, a Tory minister, and eventually the Prime Minister of Great Britain. He was a patron of both arts and sciences, and accumulated one of the finest collections of 17th-century Dutch paintings, some of which hang in Mount Stuart today. The Earl's patronage of architects, Robert and John Adam led to their building his English seat, Luton Park, and to their supplying Mount Stuart with some rather grand marble jambs for the hearths.

Writer and traveller, Thomas Pennant, wrote of Mount Stuart in his *Tour of Scotland*, 'a modern house with a handsome front and wings; the situation very fine, on an eminence in the midst of a wood, where trees grow with as much vigour as in the more Southern parts – and Throstles, and other birds of song, fill the groves with their melody'.

Over the years various additions were made to the house, but Catherine Sinclair, a visitor of 1840, wrote of it in a very unkindly way in her book, *Scotland and the Scotch*. Although she was complimentary about the portraits hanging inside she wrote that the house was, 'very like a dilapidated barrack, greatly requiring a few touches of the trowel from some skilful architect...'.

The 4th Earl, who was created the Marquess of Bute in 1796, married twice. His first wife was the daughter of Viscount Windsor and Baron Mountjoy, who had great estates in South Wales. His second was the daughter of wealthy banker, Thomas Coutts. It was however this grandson, the 2nd Marquess, who created the family fortunes by developing those Welsh interests, including the building of the docks in a little place called Cardiff. It was the 2nd Marquess who first introduced Crichton into the Stuart name.

John Patrick Crichton-Stuart, the 3rd Marquess of Bute, was a deep thinker and Oxford scholar, but he will be remembered locally as the Stuart who betrayed the faith. In 1868, when he came of age he converted to Catholicism, causing anguish to his parents and stirring up the wrath of Bute's islanders. The 3rd Marquess spent his life trying to win back the affections of those he had alienated. He spent a good deal of time and money restoring the island's relics, including St Blane's and Rothesay Castle's moat.

It was ten o' clock on the 3rd of December 1877: The Marquess had been staying at the Thomas Hotel in London when the telegram came. An onlooker had reported smoke billowing out of the main building's attic. Then there was a flash, a bright tongue of flame. Within minutes a fire raged through the whole building. The extinguishing apparatus was found to be useless and the authorities were requested to help. Help also came from an unlikely source, the crew from *HMS Jackal*, which had been sailing down the Firth of Clyde at the time.

When the embers died, the house had been gutted. At first the Marquess had asked top Scottish architect, Sir Robert Rowan Atkinson to look into the restoration of the blackened shell, but eventually the two embarked upon the design of a completely new building. What they agreed upon was a magnificent five-storey Gothic palace built with old red sandstone. It would be complete with towers and turrets and would have a sixty-foot square central hall with marble columns and arches.

The construction started in 1880 with the building of a railway from the little harbour at Kerrycroy to the site. This would take the sandstone imported from the Bute works in South Wales via Cardiff docks. Though not finished, the house was ready for habitation in 1886, and was the first in Scotland to have electricity. In 1896 work began on a chapel whose lantern was modelled on that of Zaragoza Cathedral, but the Marquess never saw its completion, for in 1900 he died suddenly. Although his widow had some of the work continued, many of the planned extensions were never carried out.

The chapel, bright with white marble features, was finally finished in 1998 under the supervision of the 7th Marquess of Bute, who was known to many as Johnny Dumfries, the ex Formula One racing driver. The 7th Marquess also opened the house and gardens to the public.

Today as you stand in the central hall and look up through the classical marble columns and arches to the stained glass windows of the upper floors and beyond to the vaulted roof some 80ft above your head, you cannot but be impressed by the sight that would grace any great cathedral. You climb the stairs to enter rooms clad in oak, decorated with pictures by old masters and with ornate crystal chandeliers hanging from coffered ceilings. The musty smell of floor to ceiling antiquarian books comes from the library. Mount Stuart is a temple to good taste, learning and fine living. The theme is continued in the park-like gardens, where you can wander for hours.

Eun (the point of the birds), overlooks a lonely whitewashed lighthouse, and the ruins of an old inn lie just back from the shoreline. Not far from the inn are the even older remains of a bronze-age cairn.

Above the bay, the hanging valley of **Glen Callum** delves deep into the southern ridges. Its pale mosses are best viewed from the hill, Suidhe Chatain. In a shallow glen, just east of Glen Callum is Loch na Leighe, a fine lake, whose fringes are crammed with bogbean and yellow waterlilies. Several more rocky bays line Bute's southern end, and all are worth exploring, but the ruins of **St**

Blane's Chapel and an old monastery hide in a high shaded hollow in hills just a mile to the northwest (see page 109). For visitors not wanting a long walk, there's a very narrow country lane leaving the A844 just west of Kingarth and ending at a small car park.

St Blane is thought to have been born on Bute, sometime in the 6th century. After being educated and taking his holy orders at Bangor in Ireland, Blane travelled to Rome. He returned to Bute and founded the monastery here. Viking raiders destroyed St Blane's original monastery, and the chapel you see today belongs to the 12th century and has a fine Norman arch. If you follow the cliffs northward you'll come across a huge circular structure known as the Devil's Cauldron. Many theories exist, but it probably predates the monastic buildings by some considerable time.

While you're at this end of the island, it's well worth taking a look at the rugged coastline at **Dunagoil Head**, where great cliffs of columnar basalt look down on rough coastal fields and sandstone rocks. There's a basalt dyke here too, formed when molten lava squeezed through cracks in the overstretched surface layer. From May the grasses of the foreshore may be flecked with the pink and purple of the spotted orchid and early purple orchid, meadow cranesbill and, in the wetter places, the marsh lousewort. Later, the blues of the harebell and scabious will be a common site. Beyond the cliffs of Dunagoil Head and the sea, the peaks of Arran steal some attention, but fascinating ancient history lies nearer to hand.

High on the promontory ahead are the remnants of a large-scale Bronze Age community that lived here for several centuries. Little **Dunagoil Fort** stands on the nearest of the crags overlooking the bay. It's small, and was almost certainly used as a lookout tower. Next to it, protected by the tall cliffs of the head, is the main fort, whose walls have fascinated historians for years. They have been vitrified, that is, the stones have been fused together by immense heat. The first to notice this phenomenon was early travel writer, Thomas Pennant, on his visit to Tor Doun, Fort Augusta in 1769. Some believe that the walls were manufactured this way by lacing them with timber, which would then be burned: others say it was accidental, and that invading soldiers would have carried out the burning.

Excavations of the larger site, carried out between 1915 and 1925, revealed a great deal about the community. Inside the villagers would have lived in clay and wattle huts. They had an ore furnace and casting moulds to fashion implements and weapons out of bronze and iron; and they made pottery and jewellery. These people were hunters and they went to fish in boats – facts known as the bones of red deer, wild boar and oxen and those of deep-sea cod were unearthed. The foundations of medieval longhouses suggested that the community lasted until about 1300AD (you'll see some prominent foundations in rough fields northeast of the little fort). They would have had strong links with St Blane's monastery, which nestled in the hillside above. The serfs that worked the land and tended the cattle at the monastery may well have lived in huts at the fort.

Things to See
Around Rothesay

First stop should always be the **Winter Garden** on the Victoria Street promenade. This 1920s' Grade A listed building of iron and glass now houses a restaurant and the extensive tourist information centre where you can pick up all the leaflets and guidebooks you need. It's surrounded by palm trees and in summer a colourful array of roses and bedding plants. You can play a relaxing round of putting here too.

The **Victorian Toilets** (gents only) by the harbour have been restored to their former glory after years of neglect. Pay 10p to see the tiled mosaic floors, shiny copper pipework and glass sided cisterns – you even get to use the place should the need arise!

The **Old Mansion House**, a 17th-century town house was built on the High Street by a wealthy businessman for his own needs, but ended up being taken over by the Stuarts when Rothesay Castle

Loch Fad and the hire boats (Bute)

St Ninian's Bay with the mountains of Arran behind (Bute)

Sunset over Ettrick Bay (Bute)

Bull Loch, near Black Hill (Bute)

Scalpsie Bay (Bute)

The harbour, Rothesay (Bute)

Mount Stuart (Bute)

Inchmarnock from near St Ninian's Bay (Bute)

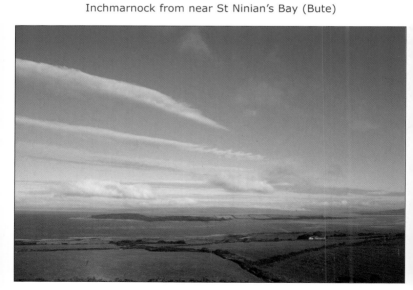

Remains of Kelspoke Castle above Kilchattan Bay (Bute)

St Michael's Grave, Kilmichael (Bute)

Kyles of Bute, near Clate Point, Glecknabae (Bute)

Kames Castle, near Port Bannatyne (Bute)

The harbour, Millport (Great Cumbrae)

Cathedral of the Isles, Millport (Great Cumbrae)

On the top of Barbay Hill, looking towards Largs and the North Ayrshire coast (Great Cumbrae)

Millport seafront (Great Cumbrae)

was burned down. The whitewashed four-storey building is still used by the Stuarts today, as their estate office.

The 13th-century **St Mary's Chapel** was in medieval times the parish church of Rothesay and served as Cathedral to the Isles in the 17th century. Now in ruins in the grounds of the High Kirk, the chapel has much of historical interest, including the tomb of Marjorie, first wife of Walter the High Steward, father to the first Stewart king, Robert II.

Bute Museum

Run by volunteers from the Buteshire Natural History Society, the Bute Museum offers valuable insights into the archaeology, history and natural history of the island. There are exhibits from Neolithic times, such as the Inchmarnock necklace and archaeological finds from some of the island's tombs. You'll also see a fascinating collection of old photographs that show how Rothesay looked at the turn of the century, some of its old trams and steam ships, many island action pictures from the World Wars, and the great harbour fire of 1962. There are special hands-on displays for children and a souvenir shop with a good selection of guidebooks. Guided walks are undertaken on Tuesdays and Thursdays throughout the summer.

Bute Natural History Museum, Stuart Street, Rothesay. Open: April-September Monday-Saturday 1030-1630 and Sunday 1430-1630.

Rothesay Castle

Rothesay Castle looks peaceful these days, set well back from the harbour and surrounded by a freshwater moat with the occasional duck for a visitor. But this proud fortress has seen a lot of action in wars between the Scots and the Vikings, then the Stewarts and the English.

There's been a castle of some sort here since the 11th century, probably built for Norse warrior, Magnus Barelegs. After the Battle of Largs the castle was handed over to the Stewarts. When King Robert II of Scotland moved here Rothesay Castle would have been a fairly primitive circular building with four round towers. In the early 16th century, James IV planned and started many improvements, including the building of the great square gatehouse tower. James V completed them before adding a chapel dedicated to St Michael within the walls. By now life in the castle would have been more luxurious, though not by today's standards. A pigeon house in the northwest ensured a supply of fresh meat in the awkward winter months, and the ladies would have had a their own comfortable parlour overlooking the courtyard.

After the occupation by Oliver Cromwell's troops in 1659 the castle was left badly damaged, but it was rendered uninhabitable after being burned down by Archibald the 9th Duke of Argyll and his Argyll Highlanders in 1685. Rothesay Castle would never again be occupied, and the Stewarts moved to the nearby Mansion House.

The years following the Napoleonic Wars were hard ones for Rothesay, and in 1816 the 2nd Marquess of Bute employed over a hundred men to clear the now tangled undergrowth and tidy up the walls from the castle's courtyard. In 1872, the 3rd Marquess had the moat cleared and undertook more restoration of the walls. He also had the Great Hall rebuilt in dressed red sandstone. Some of the artefacts found in the process – cannonballs, spears, swords and arrowheads – can now be seen in the Bute Museum. The castle, now run by Historic Scotland, is open to visitors all year round and is floodlit at night (see also page 79).

Open: (summer) 0930-1830 daily; (winter) 0930-1630 but closed on Thursday afternoons, Friday and Sunday mornings. Tel: 01700 502691.

Rothesay Creamery

See demonstrations of cheese being made.

Rothesay Creamery, The Creamery, Townhead, Rothesay PA20 9JH. Open: May-August, 1100-1500. Tel: 01700 503186.

Ascog Hall Fernery and Garden

This former Victorian fernery of Alexander Bannatyne Stewart was restored in 1997 with the planting of over a hundred ferns from all over Europe, South East Asia, Australasia, the Pacific Islands, Mexico and South America. Many species were transferred from the Royal Botanic Gardens in Edinburgh. One fern surviving from the original collection is a Todea Barbara from New Zealand, believed to be 1,000 years old. The ferns are kept in a sunken building with a glazed iron roof. This, and Bute's mild climate, keep the plants warm enough without additional Buteheating. There's a small visitor car park inside the gates of Ascog Hall.

Open: Mid April to mid October: 10:00-17:00 but closed on Mondays and Tuesdays. Tel: 01700 504555.

Ardencraig Gardens and Aviary

Run by the local council, Ardencraig Gardens has magnificent and colourful summer floral displays. There's an ornamental fishpond, an aviary of exotic birds and a tearoom.

Ardencraig Gardens and Aviary, 6 Ardencraig Lane, Craigmore, Rothesay, Isle of Bute PA20 9EZ. Open: May until September, Monday-Friday, 0900-1630; Saturday and Sunday 1300-1630 – admission free.

Mount Stuart

A trip to Bute without seeing Mount Stuart, the family seat of the Stuarts of Bute, is an incomplete trip, for this is one of the most magnificent stately homes in the whole of Britain. You'll need to set aside most if not all of the day to do the place justice.

Set in 300 acres of landscaped gardens and woodland, the 19th-century Gothic mansion was built for the 3rd Marquess of Bute after the original building, which stood on the same site, had been destroyed by fire. The design was collaboration between the Marquess and architect, Sir Robert Rowand Atkinson, and reflects the Marquess's fascination with the arts, religion and all things astrological. The 80ft/25m high great Marble Hall has pillars and arches of polished marble and magnificent stained glass windows. On the wall behind the Marble Hall Arcade hangs a huge Scottish tapestry, the Lord of the Hunt, designed by William Skeoch Cumming. Though they were commissioned in 1912, the original weavers of the tapestry were killed in the First World War, and the intricate work was only finished in 1924.

The other main rooms radiate from the hall, with their entrances on each corner. In most of these rooms hang paintings; masterpieces of portraiture by Sir Joshua Reynolds and Allan Ramsay. The wood panelled dining room is princely, with its long table and ornate glass chandeliers, but perhaps the most imposing of all the private quarters is the drawing room, which was originally intended to be three rooms, each with its own fireplace. In the end, the room was divided by two screens of marble columns and arches, an idea borrowed from Robert Adam. The Horoscope Room has an ornate astrological ceiling that depicts the position of the planets on the day of the 3rd Marquess's birth. Usually seen last on a visit, the chapel is light and airy, with brilliant white marble walls that take the eyes upwards to the high octagonal lantern, which was modelled on that of La Seo Cathedral, Zaragoza.

Though there's a regular courtesy bus running from the visitor centre to Mount Stuart's house, many people prefer to walk through the gardens and woods. The nice people at the centre will give you a helpful map with walks and information.

The gardens were laid out by the 3rd Earl, a keen botanist who had helped set up the Botanical Gardens at Kew. The first place you come to is the Kitchen Garden. This was redesigned in 1990 by Rosemary Verey for the 6th Marquess. Here flowers fruit trees and vegetables have been planted together: against one wall you have plum and damson trees co-existing with sage and lavender. In the centre stands the Pavilion, bought from the Glasgow Garden Festival in 1988. The modern glass and aluminium structure is heated to create an environment for tropical and subtropical plants from the mountain ranges of Papua New Guinea, Borneo, South America and New Zealand. Among the plants are rare orchids, passion flowers, hibiscus and a carnivorous pitcher plant.

There are four designed walks through the gardens. The shortest is the 1-mile (1.6km) Pinetum Walk, which passes through conifers that include giant redwoods from America, Western Hemlock and Douglas Fir. The longest, the Kerry Trail is 3¹/₂ miles (5.6km) and includes a stroll by the shoreline to Kerrycroy. In amongst the trees you'll come across a tall Doric column topped by a statue of Augusta, the mother of George III. It was originally raised in the grounds of Luton Park by the 3rd Earl, whose admiration for the lady is illustrated by the inscription from Virgil's *The Aeneid*: 'Dum Memor ipse mei dum spiritus hos regit artus', which means 'You will remain in my memory so long as I am conscious and my spirit controls my limbs'.

In these beautiful grounds there are many quiet places where you could picnic, or explore the wonderfully laid-out garden corners, where colourful trailing plants flow down sandstone rocks next to pretty waterfalls shaded by copper-coloured Japanese acer trees, but the best thing is for you to see them for yourselves (see also page 92).

Open: Easter Weekend, then May to the end of September. Closed Tuesdays and Thursdays. Gardens open: 1000-1800; House 1100-1700. For guided garden tours. Tel: 01700 502016. For winter house tours. Tel: 01700 503877.

St Blane's Chapel

Tucked away in a grassy hollow on the craggy south-west side of the island, the monastic site of St Blanes dates back to the 6th century, when Blane, the Celtic monk came over from Ireland. Though much of St Blane's original monastery has gone, the tall cashel walls are remarkably intact. To the left, under the cliffs, are the remains of the manse, where the minister would have lived, then there are two graveyards, the lower one for the womenfolk and the upper one, for the men of the parish: very politically incorrect, but a common practice in early Christian burial grounds. In the lower burial ground you'll see some foundations, which some archaeologists believe to be Blane's original chapel. The chapel you see today is medieval, dating back to the 12th century. The Norman rounded arch would have been built when the Nave was added.

To get to St Blanes take the A844 out of Rothesay past Ascog and Mount Stuart. Beyond Kingarth take the minor road on the left. There's a place for a few cars in a small car park at the termination of the road proper near the Plan Farm. The waymarked route takes only a few minutes.

St Ninian's Chapel

There's less to see here, though the situation is magnificent. The grassed-over foundations of this 6th-century chapel lie on a grassy spit between two stony bays, with Arran's peaks forming a backdrop. Next door to the chapel you'll see the more substantial ruins of an old kippering shed where herrings were smoked.

To get to the chapel from Rothesay take the B878 past Greenan

Loch, keep straight ahead to follow the westbound A844, then at a sharp right-hand bend turn off on a narrow road signposted to Straad. From here it's just a short walk to the bay.

Kilmichael Chapel

Kilmichael Chapel is just one of many ancient monuments to be found on the northwest side of Bute, and I recommend visitors to buy the Nature Trail No. 4 by the Buteshire Natural History Society to discover the region for themselves. The chapel and the surrounding Neolithic settlements can only be reached on foot.

Dedicated to the 6th-century St Maccaile, the ruin contains the stone altar and aumbrey (a recess for storing church vessels). On the south side the chapel walls have been built over the remains of a Bronze Age cyst.

To get to the chapel from Rothesay take the A886 past Port Bannatyne and Kames before taking the left fork (A844) then the right fork B875 to Ettrick Bay. A narrow cul-de-sac road with passing places leads to the car park at Glecknabae where the walk along a stony track begins.

Things to Do

Cinema

The Winter Garden – 1 screen
Open: daily. Tel: 08707 200219.

Golf

Rothesay Golf Course, on Canada Hill is a parkland course with a splendid elevated position overlooking Rothesay Bay and the Kyles of Bute. It boasts a modern, licensed clubhouse and a well-stocked professional's shop. Booking is advisable for weekend play.
Holes: 18; Length: 5,935 yards; Par: 69. **Facilities**: *Use of clubhouse, including bar, changing room and showers. Bar food available. Trolley and club hire available. Tel: 01700 503554.*

Bute Golf Club, at Stravanan Bay east of Kingarth is a remote seaside links course of 9 holes, with wonderful views across the bay to the peaks of Arran.
Holes: 9; Length: 2,497 yards; Par: 68 (round twice). **Facilities**: *Use of clubhouse,*

including changing room and showers. No access Saturday mornings. Tel: 01700 504369.

Port Bannatyne Golf Club is a hillside golf course looking over the town to the Kyles of Bute and Kames Bay.
Holes: 13; Length: 4,623 yards (you play the first 5 holes twice); Par: 68, Facilities: Use of clubhouse, including bar, changing room and showers. Bar food available. Tel: 01700 504544.

Fishing
Sea Angling
The warm waters of the Firth of Clyde make sea angling from Bute's rocky shoreline a rewarding activity, and you can take a boat out from Rothesay pier too for a wide range of catches, from mackerel, sea trout, flounder, plaice and dogfish to conger eels.

Freshwater Fishing
The natural **Loch Fad**, southwest of Rothesay, is well stocked with both Rainbow and Brown trout. There are thirty 14ft 4HP outboard motorboats for hire. The site has facilities for the disabled. Various competitions are held here each year, including the Troutmaster, Sunday Post and Autumn Doubles. Fishing lessons are available and rods can be hired, but they must be pre-booked.
Enquiries: Loch Fad Fisheries Ltd, Isle of Bute PA20 9PA. Tel: 01700 504871. Permits available from bailiff's hut at the Lochside.

You can also hire boats on the shallow Quien Loch, which is just inland from the west coast at Scalpsie Bay. It's fly-fishing only here for brown trout, which average between one and two pounds in weight.

Loch Ascog, south of Rothesay, is a must for those who prefer coarse fishing. Pike of up to 20lb and perch up to 3lb are regularly caught here. There are also roach in the lake. The shallow, reedy **Greenan Loch** lies just off the Rothesay-Straad road. Here you can catch common and crucian carp, tench, bream and roach.

NOTE: course fish caught from Loch Ascog and Greenan Loch should be returned unharmed to the water.
Enquiries for the Quien, Ascog and Greenan Lochs to Bute Art and Tackle, Rothesay (Tel: 01700 5035980).

Sailing

The Firth of Clyde and the Kyles of Bute have long been regarded as some of the finest sailing waters in Britain: they're certainly some of the most scenic. Many events are held each year: some one-offs, others annual.

Berthing

The pontoon berthing at Rothesay Pier is convenient for the town's centre. Showers are available at the nearby Victorian toilets. For availability telephone Rothesay Harbour on VHF channel 12 or 16 otherwise ring the numbers below:

Rothesay Berthing. Tel: 01700 500630; Mobile: 07787 365104.

The pontoons at Rothesay are supplemented by moorings in Rothesay Bay, Kilchattan Bay and Port Bannatyne.

Royal Rothesay Regatta

This annual mid-June event includes the Round Bute Yacht Race for the Marquess of Bute Trophy. All classes of yachts are allowed to enter. There are inshore races for dinghies and keelboats.

Enquiries: Malcolm Johnston. Tel: 01700 502891; Email: Malcolm@isle-of-bute.com.

Bute Sailing School

This sailing school offers RYA approved sailing courses, theme cruises as well as yacht and skipper charter.

Bute Sailing School, Cannon House, Battery Place, Rothesay, Isle of Bute PA20 9DP. Tel: 01700 502819; Email: butesail@clara.net; Website: www.butesail.com.

Diving

There are many dive sites in the area with wrecks off Cumbrae, Arran and the Ayrshire coast, including Bennan Head, Ailsa Craig, Ardrossan and Troon.

Contact: Anthony Wass. Tel: 01294 833724.

Boats can be chartered from Flying Eagle Charters, Largs Yacht Haven, Largs, North Ayrshire (Tel: 01294 469294).

Swimming

Rothesay Leisure Pool

The 25-metre pool has a beach area, sauna and solarium, private showers, and a fitness suite.

Rothesay Leisure Pool, High Street, Rothesay. Open: daily from 10:00. Tel: 01700 504300.

Cycling

Bute is ideal for cyclists, with its quiet roads that wind through picturesque countryside, through the mountains, forests and woods, and along the coast. The unsurfaced Moor Road across Scoulag Moor west of Mount Stuart, and the forest tracks in the north of the island are particularly good off-road cycling routes.

The **Bute Wheelers** is an active cycling club that promotes many events and races for all levels of competitor, including the Isle of Bute Cycling Festival held each September. The bike shop in Rothesay also arranges a mid-summer Mountain Bike Challenge that attracts competitors from far and wide.

Bicycles, both mountain and road versions, can be hired from The Mountain Bike Centre, East Princess Street, Rothesay. Tel: 01700 502333.

Horse Riding

The quiet country lanes and woodland tracks are also perfect for equestrians, as are the sandy beaches. Bute has two riding centres that cater both for novices and the experienced:

Kingarth Trekking Centre & School Complex, offers riding holidays, mini-breaks, hourly and day rides.
Tel: 01700 831673 (daytime), 01700 831255 or 831627 (evenings).

The Rothesay Riding Centre, Ardbrannan, Canada Hill, Rothesay offer 1- or 2-hour lessons or half- or full-day rides. They also arrange weekly riding holidays.
Tel: 01700 504971.

Walking

Though it has none of Arran's high mountains or wild glens, walking on Bute has its own appeal. In the north the heather hills feel a lot more remote than they are in reality, for there are so few inhabitants – just deer, grouse and birds of prey. In the south the hills are lower but studded with crag, and the coastal paths are as good as anything Arran has to offer. Bute has its own middle-distance path, The West Island Way. Opened in 2000, it's a 30-mile waymarked walk that is easy enough for non-seasoned walkers to do, perhaps in two or three days.

Walk 1: Kilchattan and St Blanes Chapel
Distance: 4¹/₂ miles (7km); Height gain: 790 feet (240m);
Time: allow 3 hours

This is undoubtedly the finest walk on the island, offering a splendid mix of rugged coastline, a hill with a whole-island view, and a monastic site of great historical importance. If you're in the car, drive through Kilchattan to the end of the road then down go through the gate onto the rough track to reach the small car park about 100yds/m further on. The path that you follow is part of the West Island Way and will be waymarked as such.

From the car park, continue along the coastal track, out along the grassy foreshore and beneath the cliffs of Hawks Neb. As the path approaches Rhubh 'an Eun it divides. Take the upper right fork, which gives you a fine view over Glencallum Bay and its lighthouse.

After dropping down to the bay the path climbs round the next headland before descending right to the west shores of Loch na Leighe, a rush-lined loch with a small island in the middle. To the north of the loch you join a farm track heading towards the Plan (farm). Just short of the farm a waymarker highlights the path that goes right to cross a footbridge over a burn. Turn left to climb the pastured spur up to St Blanes.

In a grassy hollow shaded by trees and crags, you'll see the walls of St Blane's Monastery and the ruins of a 12th-century chapel (see page 109). Beyond the complex turn right, through a gate to join a rough track climbing the bracken-cloaked hillsides to the north. Go over a stile at the top of the track and climb by the fence directly towards the rounded hill of Suidhe Chatain. The path eventually bypasses the summit to the right, but it's worth detouring up the last steep slopes to see the view. Both sides of the island can be seen, as can the whole expanse of the Firth of Clyde. The path proper continues by the edge of some woodland, before entering them near the bottom. A winding woodland track now takes the route down to the road in Kilchattan centre. Turn right to return to the car.

Walk 2: Discovering Bull Loch
Distance: 5¹/₂ miles (9km); Height gain: 650 feet (200m); Time: 2¹/₂ hours

This there and back walk is also part of the West Island Way, but leaves the main route to seek out a small mountain loch. The best place to park your car is by the Colintraive ferry. It's just a short walk back down the road to the start of the path by Rhubodach Cottage. Go through the gate and follow the rough track up into the forest. Double-back right at the next junction of tracks.

The route is undulating and you get glimpses of the Kyles of Bute through the trees. Ignore the track down to Balnakailly, but instead follow the main track, which swings southwards round Sight Hill. Turn right off the track to follow a path along a forest ride.

After leaving the forest, a narrow but well-defined path continues across heather moors, rounding the south side of Ronald's Hill. The path fades out as it reaches the marshy hollow surrounding the lake, but there are plenty of picnic spots on the rocks above. It's quite a rough and pathless trek to the top of Ronald's Hill, but the views of the Kyles make it a worthwhile if you're fit and well-shod.

Other good walking itineries include:
Barone Hill and Kirk Dam above Rothesay, to see the site of a Neolithic fort where the islanders gathered stones to attack the English who were holding Rothesay Castle.

Skipper Woods (Bogany Wood on the maps) **and Canada Hill**, Rothesay – Picturesque views over Rothesay Bay.

The Garrison Road above Port Bannatyne – short walk giving fine views over Kames Bay.

Ettrick Bay to Kilmichael – an easy walk to see numerous ancient burial sites and settlements.

Across the Island the short way – across fields from Kilchattan to Stravanan Bay

All these walks and more can be followed using the Isle of Bute-A map Guide to Eight Easy to Follow Walks (Footprint).

Tours
Bus Tours
Between the end of June and the third week in September Stagecoach Western operate a Grand Island Tour on an open-topped bus. There are three a day, and they last about 1¹/₂ hours. Buy your ticket from the driver.
Stagecoach Western Buses. *Tel: 01700 502076.*

Car Tours
Tour 1: Port Bannatyne, Ettrick Bay and Straad, Loch Fad
From Guildford Square by the harbour go up Victoria Street, past the Winter Garden and the Pavilion and follow the main coastal road round Rothesay Bay. Just beyond the sailing club and Skeoch Woods, take the right fork, Marine Place, which stays on the coast and into the centre of Port Bannatyne.

At the far end of the village turn left along the A844 to Ettrick Bay. In fields to the right you'll see Kames Castle, while to the left among some gaunt trees are some ancient standing stones. Take the next right fork, the B875 signposted to Ettrick Bay. There's a good car park by the Ettrick Bay Tearoom and the sandy beach.

Beyond the tearooms the B884 turns into a narrow unclassified road with passing places. Follow it to the road-end at Glecknabae for a short walk to Kilmichael, or you can just amble by the local seashore. Return to Ettrick Bay and the junction with the A844. This time turn sharp right. The road passes the south side of Ettrick Bay and heads south. At a junction and a sharp left-hand bend turn right along the road signposted to Straad. The narrow cul-de-sac ends at the hamlet. It's only a short way to the picturesque beach at St Ninian's Bay.

Return to the A-road and follow it eastwards for a mile. Where the A-road turns right leave it for the B878 which passes Greenan Loch on its way back to Rothesay. Just outside Rothesay, it's worth detouring right following the lane down to Loch Fad's shores – a narrow road with passing places.

What you'll see:
Port Bannatyne, Kames Castle, Kilmichael, Ettrick Bay, St Ninian's Bay and church (ruins), Greenan Loch, Loch Fad.

Tour 2: Kingarth, Kilchattan, Scalpsie Bay and Loch Fad

From Guildford Square follow Albert Place, past the yacht pontoons, then continue along East Princes Street and Battery Place round the south side of the Bay. If you want to see the Ardencraig Gardens and its aviary turn right along Albany Road just beyond the pier at Craigmore.

Turn left for a few yards at the T-junction then right along Eastlands Road. Ardencraig is the first on the left. Otherwise, continue along the coastal road, which beyond Bogany Point swings south. Ascog Hall Fernery lies to the right, a mile and a half from Bogany Point, and just beyond the square towered church at Ascog Point (left).

The road turns inland beyond the neat estate village of Kerrycroy, and passes the entrance to Mount Stuart. At the next junction, keep with the main road by taking the right fork, which descends to a crossroads by the Kingarth Hotel. Follow the road slightly right of straight ahead. It takes you down to the beach at Kilchattan Bay where there's some fine coast walking.

Return to Kingarth, turn left at the hotel, then left again by a cemetery and spruce wood, down an unclassified and narrow tarmac lane with passing places. After 2 miles (3km) the road comes to a small car park used for visiting St Blane's Chapel.

After returning to the cemetery, turn left along the A844, then left again at the junction with the B881 (Loch Fad, Rothesay Road), and follow the road to the car park (right) in the quarry beneath Tarmore Hill. Here you can take a short walk to Scalpsie Bay, the best place on Bute to view seals or climb to the top of the hill. Turn left out of the car park, but this time go left to follow the B881 past Loch Fad.

As you re-enter Rothesay you can visit the ruins of St Mary's Chapel in the grounds of the High Kirk (on the left between the creamery and the hospital).

What you'll see:
Ascog Fernery, Ardencraig Gardens, Kerrycroy, Mount Stuart, Kilchattan Bay, St Blane's Chapel, Scalpsie Bay, Loch Fad, St Mary's Chapel.

Eating out

Rothesay
Fowlers
Fowler's bistro is deservedly the most popular eating-house in Rothesay. It's setting is the seafront side of the Winter Garden. The daily menu is crammed onto a blackboard. Whether you like seafood or steak; Italian or French, there will be something for you here – and beautifully cooked too.
Closed Monday evenings and all day Tuesday. Tel: 01700 500505.

Ardyne St Ebba
We stayed here and sampled some of the good local dishes, which include Cullen Skink (a smoked haddock soup), Loch Fad trout grilled with lemon parsley butter, or Scottish salmon steamed in raspberry vinegar. If you like your food rich, how about supreme of chicken with black pudding and a whisky sauce? The Chilean Malbec and Sauvignon Blanc house wines are very good value too!
37-38 Mount Stuart Road. Open all year: Tel: 01700 502052.

India Pavilion
If you like curries, then this is the place.
7 Argyle Street, Rothesay. Tel: 01700 504988.

Jade Garden
The restaurant has the customary goldfish tank in the corner and the fish look worried that they might end up on the menu. The food is Peking and Cantonese cuisine, and rather good; the wine is reasonably priced.
25 Gallowgate, Rothesay. Tel: 01700 502347.

The Black Bull
The oldest pub on the island, and it certainly has a good ambience and friendly service. If you want a bar meal, the inn only serves them at lunchtimes and on Saturdays.
Albert Place, Rothesay. Tel: 01700 502366.

Zavaroni's

There are several Zavaroni's cafés in Rothesay, most with an ambience dating back to 1960s' coffee bars and ice cream parlours.

Harbour Café

Just opposite the yacht pontoons – it's an Internet café with an ISDN line. If you're not into the Internet you can read a morning paper while enjoying filled French baguettes or a jacket potato with a cappuccino.

East Princes Street, Rothesay. Tel: 01700 505166.

Outside Rothesay

The Teapot Tearoom, Port Bannatyne

A pleasant café with views across Kames Bay, it offers tea or coffee with good home-baked cakes and snacks.

Open all year. Tel: 01700 503603.

The Ettrick Bay Tearoom

Looking out to the beautiful sands of Ettrick Bay, this tearoom offers a simple menu including sandwiches and filled rolls, home-made cakes and snacks.

Open all year. Tel: 01700 500223.

Kingarth Hotel

The Kingarth Hotel prides itself on being the only traditional country pub on the island. It can get busy on summer weekends, especially when the place has a wedding party booked in (which it often does). The food is good: we ate in the Smiddy Bar and had a wickedly 'rich' lamb shoulder on a redcurrant sauce. The Garden Restaurant specialises in game and seafood dishes, though there's plenty for the vegetarian. You can also eat *al fresco* in the beer garden, which surrounds a bowling green.

Open all year: Tel: 01700 831662.

St Blane's Hotel, Kilchattan Bay

The hotel is on the water's edge at Kilchattan Bay. Bar meals are served in the lounge or on the lawned front garden.

Tel: 01700 831224.

Events

Bute Highland Games

Started in 1947, the Bute Highland games is held each year in the middle of August. Programme events include Highland Dancing to traditional pipe bands, athletics and wrestling, including the Heavyweight Championship for the Duke of Rothesay Trophy, donated by Prince Charles.

Enquiries: to the Tourist Information Centre, Rothesay (Tel: 01700 502151) or Bute Highland Games c/o Gordon Sutherland, Honorary Secretary, Birgidale, Kingarth, Isle of Bute PA20 9PE. Tel: 01700 831610.

Isle of Bute Jazz Festival

This popular festival is now one of the top UK traditional jazz events on the calendar.

Usually held on May Day Bank Holiday weekend Thursday evening to Monday afternoon.

Enquiries: Isle of Bute Jazz festival, 4 Ettrickdale road, Port Bannatyne, PA20 0QZ. Tel: 01700 502800.

Isle of Bute International Folk Festival

This is held in the middle of July each year.

Enquiries: Tourist Information Centre, Rothesay (Tel: 01700 502151) or Isle of Bute International Folk Festival, c/o Gillie Banks, 1 St Blanes Terrace, Kilchattan, Isle of Bute PA20 9NN. Tel: 01700 831614 or email gillie@butefolk.freeserve.co.uk.

Rothesay Royal Regatta

See listing under sailing (page 112).

The Island of Great Cumbrae

In Gaelic, the word 'Cumbray' means refuge, and it's a fitting name for this lovely pastoral island, just off the North Ayrshire Coast. Though it is not much more than a mile from the mainland, Great Cumbrae feels like it's a million miles from the stress of modern Britain, its traffic jams and its fast-moving pace of life.

The stretch of water between the ferry quay at Largs to the concrete slipway on Great Cumbrae is so narrow that you can see quite clearly the little single-decker bus that's coming to pick up the foot passengers and whisk them away along the winding coast road to the hidden village of Millport.

It takes the little roll-on roll-off ferry ten minutes to sail across. **Millport** still hides in a bay to the south: the bus heads south to seek it out. To get the best views, sit on one of the nearside seats. Great Cumbrae's not so great in size: it's about 4 miles (7km) long by 2 miles (3km) at its widest point, and the bus will take a very short while indeed to get you to the south side of the island.

Through the window, your first notable views are back across the firth to Largs, where the sandstone-spired church is backed up by the rolling hills of Muirshiel. Soon you'll see canoes on the water and the brightly coloured sails of dinghies – there's a good watersports instruction centre here.

Just to the south, there's an old walled pier and the pretty whitewashed **Downcraig Ferry House**, which, in days gone by, was an inn, catering for thirsty travellers who had just got off the boat. Now it's a holiday cottage. The house is named after Dun Creag, which means the crag of the fort, and refers to the vitrified fort on the hill. By the pier there's **Haco's Mound**. A local legend says that Norse King, Haco or Haakon stood on this spot and watched in horror as his fleet was decimated by the great storms that raged during his defeat at the Battle of Largs in 1263.

Beyond the beach at Ballochmartin Bay the little bus rounds

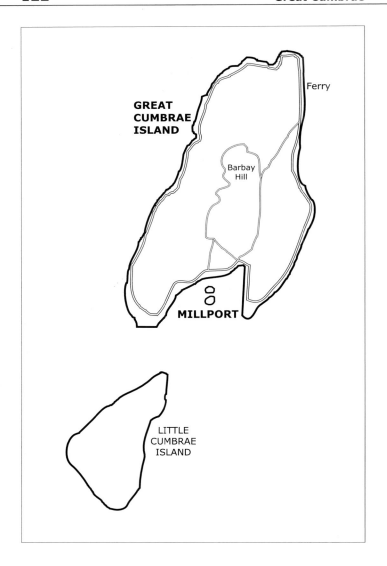

Clashfarland Point and the road continues in the shadow of Clashfarland Hill's steep grassy slopes. A strangely shaped rock juts out from these slopes. It's 30ft (10m) high by 12ft (4m) wide and a huge 165ft (50m) long, it is known as **The Lion**. The rock is one of many basalt dykes, formed in the Tertiary period of volcanic activity, when molten rock was squeezed through cracks in the overstretched upper crust. Unfortunately a crack has developed that in 2001 threatens to sever the lion's head, and the islanders have set up an appeal to raise £15,000 for remedial work to halt the damage. This was completed in November 2001.

The little pier at **Keppel** is overwhelmed by the enormous piers and buildings of the Hunterston Deep Water Terminal, which stretches halfway across the firth from the North Ayrshire Coast. But it's not long before the road turns its back to Ayrshire, rounds the hill and traces the foot of sandstone cliffs into Millport Bay. The bay is deeply indented and sheltered, with the whitewashed cottages and shops of Millport and the sandy beach stretching out for over a mile from the red cliffs of Ninian Brae to the far promontory at Portachur Point. The spire of the cathedral looks over the scene, topped only by pinewoods and the pastured Sheughand Hills. A score of sailing boats are anchored in the bay, most of them not far from the squat rocky islets known simply as the Eileans. Beyond them the precipitous sides of Little Cumbrae lead the eye across the waves to the distant peaks of Arran's Sleeping Warrior.

Past a row of brightly coloured terraced cottages, the road swings left round the sandy Kames Bay and heads for the village centre. The harbour is small, and rather like one you'd find in a Cornish fishing village. Overlooking it there's the Royal George Hotel, looking a little weather-beaten as a fishing village's pub is expected to be. Beyond the harbour there's a larger pier for the fishing boats. The aromas of fish and chips from a nearby take-away mingle in the breezes with the salt and seaweed. And while the cormorants out in the bay are happy to catch their own fish, the noisy seagulls that circle overhead, are ready to pounce on yours, should you be careless enough to take your eyes off them for a second.

The star attraction of Millport is its beach – one that is safe for children, with long, flat stretches of sand. The sands are punctuated by barnacle- and muscle-covered red sandstone rocks that have been eroded into strange shapes. One, the Crocodile Rock, has been painted in red and white to resemble that fearsome reptile – inelegant but extremely popular with the children, who ride the rock like Crocodile Dundee.

In days gone by smuggling was a part of life in Millport, almost an accepted part. I have read that on one occasion Holy Communion had to be postponed because the wine hadn't been smuggled in time for the service. It's inevitable then that revenue cutters were also a part of daily life in the village too, and had been since 'the Kings Boat' went into service in 1634. In 1745, Captain Crawford of the cutter, *Royal George*, had the **Garrison House** built to house himself and his crew, some sixty men. Set back from the shore road in a splendid garden setting it was to become the pride of Millport.

The Earl of Glasgow enlarged the building in 1819 and turned it into a grand mansion along the lines of Sir Walter Scott's Abbotsford. When the Earl's fortunes collapsed, the Marquis of Bute purchased the house and his lands. The Bute Estate then became the island's major landowner and continued to be until 1999, when they allowed all the tenants to buy their own properties. In 1947, the Marquis let the house to the council on a 99-year lease. Through lack of funds the Garrison House gradually fell into disrepair, and in 1995 the council boarded up all the windows. The islanders and the council hoped that they would be able to obtain lottery funding to restore the building to former glories and to house the Museum of the Cumbraes. The decision was to be made in July 2001.

But fate was unkind to Millport. In June the building was set ablaze. It's believed that local children started the fire – they had been reported many times to the police for using the house as a den. The fire quickly took hold, and fire engines were sent from far and wide – ferried across late into the night by Caledonian MacBrayne. But it was to no avail: the building was charred and gutted. Barriers were erected to keep visitors out, and the lottery bid was postponed. The planners were back to square one, and the Museum was still looking for a home.

At the time of writing renewed rescue bids for the scheme are being planned, but the locals were not very hopeful with rumours circulating about the place being demolished. I hope that common sense will prevail and the Garrison House will be restored in a project, which surely must be ideal for a Lottery grant. (Check for progress on www.millport.net or www.millport.org.)

Walk up the hillside along College Street and you'll come to the entrance to the **Cathedral of the Isles** (see also page 128). The cathedral itself lies at the end of a long drive through woodland. Looking up at the magnificent 123ft (38m) spire you wouldn't believe it, but this is the smallest cathedral in the United Kingdom with seating for only a hundred.

The benefactor, George Frederick Boyle, 6th Earl of Glasgow, had been deeply involved in religion during his student days at Oxford in the 1840s. It was his dream to rejuvenate the Episcopal Church in Scotland. In 1849, he engaged the architect, William Butterfield to design both a church and college buildings. Butterfield would go on to design several better-known buildings, such as Keeble College, Oxford. Both church and college opened two years later. In 1876, the church became the seat of the Bishop of the Isles and accordingly, the church became a cathedral. In the 1880s, the Boyles, who had owned much of the island, lost their money and the cathedral, its benefactor.

Kirkton lays claim to the oldest ecclesiastical sites. Today, the hamlet, set in a verdant hollow to the north of the village, consists of a few houses, a campsite, a golf course, a riding school and an ancient cemetery with a few interesting crosses. At one time this was *the* most important centre of Cumbrae.

In these cemetery grounds, the Irish missionaries set up the first Christian chapel, sometime in the 7th century. It is believed that the chapel was dedicated to St Maura, who, along with Beya on 'wee' island, dedicated her later life to teaching the gospels in the

Cumbraes. The marauding Vikings probably sacked and destroyed this first chapel, during the 8th or 9th centuries.

In a statistical account of Cumbrae in 1794 it was reported that the village of Millport had sixty houses, 'most of them built within the last 25 years'. The parish church of 1612 was still up at Kirkton and it was reported to be too small at that time. The church was eventually demolished in 1837 to make way for the present one that lies down the hill.

W Lytteil in his *Guide-Book to the Cumbraes* of 1886 suggested that the settlement, which would have been Keil-Maura, had its name corrupted, first to K'umra, then to the future name of the island, Cumbrae.

If you're looking for a short evening stroll from Millport, there's a path leading from the boat yard to the shore at Portachur Point, a favoured spot for both common and grey Atlantic seals. You can often see them basking on the rocks in between forays for fish. Nearby masses of yellow flag iris add a little colour to the foreshores. The precipitous western cliffs of Little Cumbrae dominate the view across the stretch of water known as the Tan.

If you're continuing round the island you'll probably be doing so on foot, by car, or by far the best way, by bicycle. There are several bike hire shops in the village (see page 131).

North of Portachur Point the road follows the line of a raised beach formed after the last Ice Age when the ground, released from the weight of ice, sprang back, leaving a new beach 50ft (15m) below it. To your right are the old sea cliffs: to your left the new ones.

As long as it's fine and the atmosphere is clear, views across the firth to the Isle of Bute will be attracting your attention from here. Kilchattan Bay and the rocky bluffs of Bute's southern hills are no more than 3 miles (5km) away and the dusky red palace of Mount Stuart can be discerned through its wooded grounds.

At **Sheriff's Port** the shelf gets narrower, confined by the wooded cliffs on the right. The plaintive cries come from the fulmars, but don't go too close, for these birds, if disturbed, can regurgitate a very unpleasant smelling substance and their aim is true. Round the next bend you'll see a score of bicycles just off road. The cyclists are taking a break in the Fintry Bay Tearoom, perhaps Cumbrae's most popular café. If you start from the ferry terminal, it's halfway round the island. Fintry Bay is also a splendid spot for a swim or just lounging on the beach. Like Millport Bay, it's safe for the children.

Continuing north, the road comes to **Skate Point**, one of the best spots for bird watching. Here you may see eiders, gannets and terns on the water, and possibly ringed plovers and turnstones on the rocks.

Rounding the corner to the north side you come across two little sandy inlets, one with the horrible name **Stinking Bay**, the other known as **White Bay**. Lapwings nest close to the road here, so be careful not to disturb them. Beyond the second beneath the cairned knoll of Aird Hill the obelisk of the Tormont End memorial looks out to sea, and Largs comes back into view.

I've now taken you round the coast but I've saved the best bit of Cumbrae for the last. Now we'll go to **Barbay Hill**, which at 417ft (127m), is the highest place on the whole island. Take the B-road, climbing away from the shore at Dun Craig. After winding past farms it comes to a tee-junction. Turn right here, and follow a narrow country lane that climbs to lofty pastures and finally, to the top of the hill. It's just a few paces to the **Glaid Stone**… but what a view! On a clear day those with a knowledge of the Scottish peaks will be able to distinguish the Loch Lomond and the Arrochar Alps climbing into the northern sky beyond the blue waters of the Firth of Clyde and the rolling heather hills of Cowal. As usual for these parts the jagged peaks of Arran are prominent beyond the low-slung Island of Bute. It's all set out beneath your feet like a real-life map.

If you don't know these parts to well, all's not lost for there's a topograph naming all you can see – and a few you can't! When you're ready to return the bike, just continue along the road, which winds down the other side of the hill past the cathedral and back into Millport.

Thing to See

Cathedral of the Isles

Designed by William Butterfield, one of the finest architects of the Gothic revival era, in 1849, the cathedral is adjoined by two college buildings, a chapter house and a hail and cloister. The raised lawned area the buildings stand on make you look up to the sky to see the tall pyramidal steeple which belies the size of this, the United Kingdom's smallest cathedral.

Inside, the Nave is plain and very small at just 40ft by 20 (12m by 6). In contrast, the chancel with its brightly coloured tiles and impressive stained glass windows is quite ornate – note the ceiling, elegantly painted with depictions of the island's native wildflowers.

Garrison House

Along with almost every islander, I'm hoping that the once elegant Garrison House will be rebuilt sometime soon, and will, as intended, house the Museum of the Cumbraes.
Check websites www.millport.org or www.isle-of-cumbrae.net.

Robertson Museum and Aquarium

You can see a wide variety of marine life from the Clyde area here. The exhibition has interpretations of 'simple marine science'.
University Marine Biological Station, Millport KA28 0EG.
Open: Weekdays and Saturdays, Easter and June-September, 0930-1215 and 1400-1645 (1615 on Fridays). Tel: 01475 530581/2; Website: www.millport.gla.ac.uk/ Acad/Marine.

Things to Do

Cinema

The Cinema, Town Hall at Millport – 1 screen
Open in summer only. Tel: 01475 530741.

Golf

Being a small island there's just enough room for one golf course on Cumbrae. **Millport Golf Club**, formed in 1888, lies on the south-western hillslopes of the island, just above Millport.

The first few holes involve climbing over hilly countryside, but the remainder are an easy stroll across lofty grasslands. The surroundings are magnificent. As you saunter down the fairways you can look across the Firth of Clyde to the Island of Bute, and further still, to the impressive peaks of Arran and the rounded ridges of Cowal.

Though Millport is not a difficult course (there are no par fives, for example), it does have some holes to test the low-handicap golfer. For instance, there are a couple of long par threes with small greens. One or two of the par fours are quite long and there are several blind shots to pit your wits against. The 162-yard 4th hole is surrounded by six bunkers, so anything short will end in trouble.

When the wind blows from the south, Millport takes on the characteristics of a links course.

Holes: 18; *Length*: 6,000 yards; *Par: 68*. **Facilities**: *Electric or push trolleys are available for hire. Use of clubhouse, including bar, changing room and showers. You can order a three-course meal or a sandwich. Tel: 01475 530306 (Secretary); 01475 530311 (Clubhouse); 01475 530305 (Professional); Email: secretary@millportgolfclub.co.uk; Website: www.millportgolfclub.co.uk.*

Visitors, who are welcome at all times, should contact the professional for green fees and to arrange tee-off times. There's a special deal offering two rounds of golf and your meals included.

Fishing
Sea Angling

Like all the Clyde Islands the sea off Cumbrae is good for fishing, whether it be from the shore or by boat. You might hope to catch tope, rays and mackerel, but you'll possibly see dolphins or even a basking shark.

Boat charter is available from Flying Eagle Charters, Largs Yacht Haven, Largs (Tel: 01294 469294). They will call and pick you up at Millport.

Freshwater angling

There are two small reservoirs near the golf course on Great Cumbrae known as the Top Dam and the Bottom Dam. They're good for trout and fishing rights belong to the Cumbrae Angling Club (membership restricted to 30, but visitors are accepted.

Contact: Luigi Giorgetti, owner of Ritz Café, Stuart Street, Millport. Tel: 01475 530459 or Jim McFarlane, Newsagent, 15 Glasgow Street, Millport. Tel: 01475 530324.

Bait and fishing tackle can be bought from Mapes, 3-5 Guildford Street, Millport (Tel 01475 530444).

Sailing, Sea Canoeing and Windsurfing

The Sport Scotland National Centre, which is just to the south of the CalMac ferry pier, offers excellent facilities for most watersports in what is one of the most scenic situations in the British Isles. They describe the waters as safe but exhilarating, and this makes it an ideal place to learn how to sail or improve your skills. All the staff are RYA qualified, having passed all the necessary instructional awards.

For the dinghy sailors there are Sport 16s, Picos, Lasers, Buzzes, Dart 16s, RS400s and Laser 4000s. Windsurfers have the choice of Revos, Magnums and advanced boards, while kayakers can choose from Cyphurs and Capellas. The cruising fleet consists of Elan 36 and Dufour 35 boats, and for power boating an 8.1m Launch and a range of Tornado RIBs with appropriate engines. There's shore-based accommodation with catering and all waterproof clothing is supplied.

Sport Scotland National Centre Cumbrae, Isle of Cumbrae KA28 0HQ. Tel: 01475 530757; Email: enquiries@nationalcentrecumbrae.org.uk; Website: www.nationalcentrecumbrae.org.uk.

Diving

There are many dive sites in the area, with wrecks off Cumbrae itself, Ailsa Craig, Ardrossan and Troon. For more information contact Anthony Wass (Tel: 01294 833724).

Boats can be chartered from Flying Eagle Charters, Largs Yacht Haven, Largs. Tel: 01294 469294.

Horse Riding and Trekking

Millport Riding School

One-hour rides for beginners and longer ones for experienced riders, usually in the morning. Book in advance. Pony rides on the beach in the afternoons during the summer season – suitable for small children. Hats supplied.

Millport Riding School, Upper Kirkton Stables, Golf Road, Millport. Open: Monday-Saturday, all year. Tel: 01475 530689; Mobile 07990 872264.

Cycling
Cycling is the most popular sport on Great Cumbrae. Perhaps the best route is the 10¼ mile (16km) road around the island, which visits all the island's picturesque bays. There's also the summit road to Barbay Hill and the Glaid Stone 419ft (127m), but there are no good legal off-road routes.

Bike hire is available at Bremners Stores, 17 Cardiff Street, Millport. Tel: 01475 530707/530309; Mapes, 3-5 Guildford Street, Millport. Tel: 01475 530444; A T Morton, 4 Mount Stuart, Millport. Tel: 01475 530478.

Crazy Golf
There's a crazy golf course on the seafront at Millport.
Open: daily, from 1100 to 1730. Tel: 01475 530034.

Walking
The Lion Rock
Distance: 3 miles (5km); Height gain: 295 feet (90m);
Time: 1½ hours
Go over the stile in the roadside fence just a few paces north of Lion Rock. There's no path on the ground at first, but just head for the rock. The best way to see 'The Lion' is to look at it from the south side, then continue the walk climbing steeply up the north side before veering left to weave through gorse bushes onto the high grassy slopes. Turn right and follow the fence round the sides of the hill which now gives a superb panorama of Millport and its bay. The path now follows the fence northwards above the cliffs of Ninian Brae. After about half a mile (800m) turn left over a stile in a fence and walk across another field to cross some steps in a roadside wall opposite the drive of Ballykillet Farm. Turn left along the road, which descends to Kames Bay on the east side of Millport. By turning left along the coastal road you will return to the rock.

Other walks
The Tourist Information Centre provide a map and information sheet with the walks marked in yellow and there's a few brief descriptions on their website (www.millport.org). Perhaps the best one begins from the Golf Road at Kirkton and climbs the Sheughand Hills back to the little lane climbing to the summit of

the island at the Glaid Stone. There is a good chance of seeing a buzzard or a sparrow hawk here.

Open-Top Bus Tour

From July to August inclusive, you can take a sightseeing tour of the island on an open-top bus. Tickets are available from the bus itself or any railway station on the Glasgow to Largs line. The latter are inclusive of the rail fare. The buses depart from Millport Pier daily except Wednesdays at 0945, 1030, 1115, 1200, 1330, 1415, 1500, 1545 and 1630. Duration: 45 minutes.

Car Tour

The island is small and a car tour will not take very long. However, if you haven't the energy to go by bike, and the weather's not fine enough for an open-top bus tour, the car tour can be a rewarding little trip. The B898 coast road is nearly $10^1/_4$ miles (16km) and the obvious route to take. To avoid the ferry traffic, try going anti-clockwise. The route will take you past all the sand and seashell beaches and into Millport. If you want to go over the top at Millport watch out for College Street on the left (the one signposted to the Cathedral), then take the left fork at the junction. The road is narrow and winding but it offers stunning views at each turn. There's a car park by the Glaid Stone. At the next junction (the B899), the left fork will take you back to the ferry, while the right goes to Millport. On the latter route, you can visit the standing stone in the woods near Craigengour Farm, but seek permission first.

Eating out

The Royal George, Quayhead Street, Great Cumbrae

Bar meals are served in the dining room or there's a 'real pub' atmosphere with a jukebox and pool table. Caters for families.
Tel: 01475 530301.

The Tavern Bar (opposite the Crocodile Rock)

Bar meals and snacks with sing-alongs and other live entertainment.
Open Easter-October. Tel: 01475 530465.

The Kelburne Bar, Stuart Street
A friendly 'local' to drop into when you're thirsty. There's a family room at the back with a pool table.
Tel: 01475 530080.

The Newton Bar, Glasgow Street
Entertainment's the theme here with discos, karaokes and quiz nights. Bar snacks are served here – there's a childrens' menu.
Open all year. Tel: 01475 530920.

Grannie Jean's Coffee Shop
Retro 1960s décor with a selection of coffees, good home baked cakes and excellent soup.
Tel: 01475 530852.

Crocodile Chippy (opposite the Crocodile Rock)
Take-away, or eat in the café.
Tel: 01475 531111.

Minstrels Wine Bar, Cardiff Street
Good for seafood and fish dishes.
Tel: 01475 531080.

Events

Country and Western Festival
Each year Millport turns into a Wild West town with rodeos, 'shoot-outs' and four days of country and western music. It's usually held on the first week of September.
Enquiries: Tel: 01475 530748.

The Island of Little Cumbrae

Little Cumbrae is a private island. It has no ferries or excursions to it, and no plans for any. At the time of writing it's up for sale so who knows what's in store? But as you look across Millport Bay, or perhaps from Kelspoke Hill on Bute the mysterious 'wee' Cumbrae wails like a Siren to Odysseus to sail across. Today, besides the bird population, only divers and the odd sightseeing yachtsman visit it and that's a shame, for there's a good deal of history on the island.

Perhaps we're best using the words of W Lytteil to describe the landing on the wee isle:

> *"Sheannawally Point, or the point of the old cairns, is the name of the little headland which lies nearest to the pier of Millport. The distance by water from this "point of the old cairns" to the Auld Castle is not much more than a mile. It is now evident that the islet on which this old castle stands was formerly called Allinturail, that is, the islet of the noble's tower. Cravies-hole, or the creek of the devout folk, is at the north end of castle-island, and it is, at high water, a fairly good landing-place. But boats very often put in at the strand beside the farmhouse, and this is best managed when the tide is within two hours of reaching high-water mark."*

The auld castle Lytteil refers to was the one built for Sir Walter, the High Steward, father of the Scottish king, Robert II. It became a royal residence in 1375, and on many other occasions – he loved to hunt and fish from here. For many years, the Hunters of Hunterston were keepers of the castle, which was burned to the ground by Cromwell's troops in 1653, it is said as an act of revenge for the imprisonment and subsequent hanging of the Protector's correspondent, Archie Hamilton.

On the slopes above the castle lie the ruins of a 7th-century chapel dedicated to the missionary, St Beya who preached here in the 7th century. Lyttle also wrote a poem:

Far up among the rocky heights and scars
Which stud the rugged breast of Cumbrae's Isle—
Erst called 'of Santa Vey,' but 'Lesser' now—
One spot of sweetest green attracts the eye
And bids the wanderer pause. For all about
Rise terraced steeps and craggy walls of trap
Which make of it a quiet sanctuary,
And shut one off completely from the world.
A calm retreat in ancient times it was
When good St. Beya chose it for her cell,
And made it hallowed ground for evermore.
A tiny lakelet here called Gurack Mere,
Whose straightest English is the Lady Lake,
Reflects the grassy verdure of its rim
And shows, in its clear mirror, chapel walls
Which dwellers on the isle call Santa Vey.

He paints a romantic picture and one that surely should be seen. The scramble up the rocks of Lighthouse Hill looks exhilarating: the short excursion to the cairns and tumuli above Sheannawally Point, equally so.

With no roads, no cars, no fumes, no ugly housing estates, Little Cumbrae's a romantic get-away-from-it-all sort of place. Maybe Arran's Holy Island project should be repeated here.

Ailsa Craig

Hearken, thou craggy ocean-pyramids!
Give answer from thy voice-the sea-fowls' screams!
When were thy shoulders mantled in huge streams?
When from the sun was thy broad forehead hid?
How long is 't since the Mighty Power bid
Thee heave from airy sleep, from fathom dreams?
Sleep in the lap of thunder, or sunbeams,
Or when grey clouds are thy cold coverlid?
Thou answerest not, for thou art dead asleep!

John Keats

Ailsa Craig is a sleeping island volcano, a dome of granite with its sides spliced into gigantic splintered cliffs that plummet into the Firth of Clyde. It is a small island, just ³/₄ mile long (1,300m), by ¹/₂ mile (800m) wide, but, in that small space, the land rises to 1,114 feet (340m) above sea level. In the balmy summer of 1818, John Keats had been taking a walking tour of Scotland, and, on the Ayrshire coast leg, had been particularly impressed by the little island. Later, at the Kings Arms in Girvan, he was inspired to write the above sonnet.

The island's profile is impressive from all directions, but especially so from Kildonan on Arran, where it peeps through the sleepy haze behind Pladda, taking on the form of an upturned ship's hull. Known locally as 'Paddy's Milestone' due to its position halfway between Glasgow and the coast of Ireland, Ailsa Craig has long been associated with shipping. It has often been used by boat-builders as a marker for their ships' speed trials. The strange ears you'll see on the north and south ends are foghorns, which warned ships of impending danger.

In many places on the isle, columnar basaltic cliffs plunge straight into the surf, leaving Ailsa Craig with little shoreline to encourage human habitation – just a shingle bank beneath the cliffs of the south coast and a triangular 30-acre spit, where the lighthouse complex stands. But until 1981, when the lighthouse became automated, the island *has* been continuously inhabited, sometimes by just one tenant: and at others by many.

There's been a castle here since medieval times. A three-storey square keep is stunningly sited on a high shelf overlooking the lighthouse and jetty. Although the castle's exact history is sketchy, it has been in the hands of the powerful Kennedy family and the Hamiltons, who also owned Brodick Castle on Arran.

Ailsa Craig's fine microgranite, which contains the mineral, riebeckite, has proved particularly suitable for the manufacture of curling stones, and quarrying took place here until the early twentieth century. The busy scene would have been accentuated by the adjacent gasworks.

Tourists came to the island at this time. They would have been greeted by a teahouse, whose ruins are still evident today, and would have seen wide-ranging wildlife, including wild goats, rabbits, puffins, kittiwakes, gannets and many other seabirds. Unfortunately, with the tourists came rats. These rodents had a devastating effect on the wildlife, and virtually wiped out the puffin colony.

Ailsa Craig is now a protected nature reserve, and a permit is required to land on the island, but you can arrange this, and a trip from Girvan on the Ayrshire coast, by ringing either Rachael Clare (Tel: 01294 833724), or Martin McCrindle (Tel: 01465 713219). To get the most from the trip, they will usually sail you all the way round the island where you'll see mysterious caves, the 'ears' of the North and South Horns, the spectacularly dark perpendicular cliffs of the north. You'll see and hear around the western cliff-tops what is the largest colony of gannets in the Northern Hemisphere – there were nearly 23,000 nests in a survey of 1985. This famous predator is magnificent in flight as it dive-bombs the water in attempt to skewer some unsuspecting fish. Other seabirds you may spot include the kittiwake, guillemot, razorbill, and fulmar.

You will almost certainly be dropped off on the north jetty, near to the whitewashed lighthouse and its complex of buildings. The old tramway that runs along the coastal strip from the jetty would at one time have conveyed cargo between the ships and the quarries.

There's a good path to the castle, which is an excellent viewpoint for the Ayrshire coast. Those with a little more energy can continue up the hillside. They should pass Garry Loch, which Rev Roderick Lawson described in *Ailsa Craig*, a guide of 1888, as being 'bordered with a fringe of soft green moss and a luxuriant crop of marsh marigolds'. The summit has an OS trig point and a 360-degree panorama of blue sea, framed by the coastlines of Arran, Argyll and Ayrshire, and the more distant hills of Ireland.

As you wander round this magical island, the chances are that you will see the puffins – they're returning, in ever-increasing numbers, after a long absence.

Practical Information: Arran

Getting There
By air
The nearest airport to Ardrossan for (Arran) is Prestwick at 16 miles (26km). Prestwick has flights to and from Ireland, the rest of the UK and Europe. Ryanair operate budget flights from London Stanstead. ScotRail have special offers for rail travellers flying in to Prestwick.

Ardrossan is 27 miles (43km) from Glasgow International Airport.

Glasgow Prestwick Airport.
Website: www.gpia.co.uk.

Ryanair.
Website: www.ryanair.com.

By rail
There is a regular connecting rail service from Glasgow Central to Ardrossan Harbour (for the ferry), calling at Paisley Gilmore Street and Kilwinning. Glasgow has good rail links with the rest of the UK.

ScotRail
Contacts: All rail enquiries: 08457 48 49 50; Website: www.scotrail.co.uk; ScotRail Telesales: Tel: 08457 550033.

By ferry
Caledonian MacBrayne operate two ferries to Arran; one from Ardrossan and one from Claonaig on the Mull of Kintyre. The one from Ardrossan on the Ayrshire coast sails to Brodick and takes about 55 minutes (last check-in at least 30 minutes before departure). The smaller ferry from Claonaig sails to Lochranza on the island's north coast, but only operates in the summer. This takes about 30 minutes (last check-in at least 5 minutes before departure). A connecting bus runs between Claonaig and Tarbert.

Caledonian MacBrayne
Tel: 01475 650100 (general enquiries); 08705 65000 (reservations: charged at BT national long distance rate). Open: Monday-Saturday, 0830 and 1700. Ardrossan office (Tel: 01294 463470); Brodick (Tel: 01770 302166); Website: www.calmac.co.uk.

Recorded information for disrupted ferry services Tel: 08457 650050 (charged at local rate).

Getting Around
Bus/coach
An Area Transport Guide is available from the Tourist Information Centre at Brodick.

Three buses operated by Stagecoach Western Buses, collectively cover the island's entire coastal road:

Service 323: (southern route) connects Brodick and Blackwaterfoot via Lamlash, Whiting Bay and Kildonan.

Service 324: (northern route) connects Brodick and Blackwaterfoot via Corrie, Lochranza and Pirnmill.

Service 322: Brodick to Black-waterfoot goes cross-country via the String (road) and Shiskine.

You can devise a circular tour of the island by combining two of the above three services. To do so you can buy a special **Arran Rural Rover Ticket** (available on the bus).

Stagecoach Western Buses
Tel: 01770 302000.

Post buses

There are two post buses operated by the Royal Mail. They are both circular routes based on Brodick Post Office and run Monday to Saturday. The first goes via Corrie, Sannox, Lochranza, Catacol, Pirnmill, Machrie, Blackwaterfoot, thence back to Brodick using B880 (the String). The other one goes via Lamlash, Glenscorrodale, Corrie-cravie, Kilmorie, Shannochie, Kildonan, Whiting Bay, Lamlash and Brodick Ferry Terminal.

Inter-island Cruises

Cruises aboard the historic paddle steamer, Waverley are operated throughout the summer, with different itineraries that include Campbeltown, Kintyre, Dunoon, Loch Long, Largs and Rothesay. At present they call at Brodick on three days a week.
Contact: Waverley Excursions (Tel: 0141 243 2224).

Taxis

Arran Private Hire (Tel: 01770 600903); Lamlash Private Hire (Tel: 01770 600725); A C Hendy, Brodick (Tel: 01770 302274).

Tourist Information Centre
The Pier, Brodick.
Tel: 01770 302140; Fax: 01770 302395; Email: arran@ayrshire-arran.com; Website: www.ayrshire-arran.com.

Garages/Petrol Stations/Car Hire
Whiting Bay Garage Shore Road, Whiting Bay.
Open: Weekdays: 0900-1800; Saturday: 0930-1730; Sunday: 1200-1600 (summer). Closed Sundays in winter. Tel/fax: 01770 700345.

Arran Transport Ltd. (car hire only), The Pier, Brodick.
Open: Monday-Saturday: 0800-1930 (1730 in winter); Sunday: 1000-1930 (summer); Sunday: 1245-1645 (winter). Tel: 01770 302121; Fax: 01770 302123.

Invercloy Service Station (fuel only), Shore Car Park, Brodick.
Open: Monday-Saturday: 0800-1930 (1730 in winter); Sunday: 1100-1700 (May-September). Closed Sundays in winter. Tel: 01770 302774.

Blackwaterfoot Garage.
Open: Weekdays: 0830-1730; Saturday: 0900-1700; Sunday 1230-1730 (summer). Closed Sundays in winter. Tel: 01770 860277; Fax: 01770 860285.

Shops and Post Offices
Blackwaterfoot
Post office/general store.

Brodick
Large Co-op supermarket, post office, chemist, butcher, toyshop, baker, confectioner, several craft/souvenir shops, newsagents.

Corrie
Post office/general store, craft shops.

Lamlash
Supermarket, post office, chemist, butcher, craft shop, chandler/bait shop.

Lochranza
Post office/general store.

Kildonan
General store.

Kilmory
Post office/general store.

Whiting Bay
Supermarket, post office, chemist, newsagent, butcher, craft and hardware shops.

Banks
Bank of Scotland, Brodick.
Tel: 01770 892000. There is a mobile unit in operation.

Royal Bank of Scotland, Brodick
Tel: 01770 30222/302418. There is a mobile unit in operation.

Hospital
Arran War Memorial Hospital. Tel: 01770 600777.

Doctors' Surgeries
Brodick
Brodick Health Centre (Drs Kerr and Guthrie). Tel: 01770 302175.

Lamlash
Drs Tinto and Campbell. Tel: 01770 600516/600617.

Shiskine
Dr Grassie. Tel: 01770 860247.

Chemist
Brodick Pharmacy. Tel: 01770 302250.

Dentist
Mrs Tracey Russell, 6 Douglas Centre, Brodick. Tel: 01770 302320.

Optician
Mr & Mrs McAlistair, Unit 1 Douglas Centre, Brodick. Tel: 01770 302878.

Veterinary Surgeon
M J Wheeler, Lower Balmore, Brodick. Tel: 01770 302511.

Police
Lamlash Police Station. Tel: 01770 302573/4.

Churches
Church of Scotland
Brodick, Corrie, Kilmory, Lamlash, Whiting Bay, Lochranza and Shiskine.

United Reform Church
Sannox (July and August)

Free Church of Scotland
Kirk Care, Brodick

Roman Catholic
Church of Holy Cross, Brodick
(Douglas Hotel Grounds)

**Scottish Episcopal Church
(Anglican)**
St Margaret's, Whiting Bay

Maps
Ordnance Survey
Ordnance Survey Outdoor Leisure
37: Isle of Arran (1:25000 scale and
superb for walkers).

Ordnance Survey Explorer 361:
Cowal, Isle of Arran (1:25000 scale
virtually the same as the above,
which it will replace).
Ordnance Survey Landranger 69
Isle of Arran (1:50000 scale a good
touring map).

Harvey Maps
Harveys Superwalker: Arran
The whole of the island at 1:40000
scale on one side; on the other the
mountains of North Arran are
shown at 1:25000 scale – again
superb for walkers – they're water
resistant too.

Practical Information: Bute

Getting There
By air
The nearest airport is Prestwick,
which has flights to and from
Ireland, the rest of the UK and
Europe. Ryanair operate budget
flights from London Stanstead.
ScotRail have special offers for rail
travellers flying in to Prestwick.

It is 24 miles (39km) from
Glasgow International airport to the
ferry terminal at Wemyss Bay.

Glasgow Prestwick Airport.
Website: www.gpia.co.uk.

Ryanair
Website: www.ryanair.com.

By rail
There is a regular connecting rail
service from Glasgow Central to

Wemyss Bay (for ferry)
ScotRail
Contacts: All rail enquiries: 08457 48
49 50; Website: www.scotrail.co.uk;
ScotRail Telesales: Tel: 08457 550033.

By ferry
Caledonian MacBrayne run two
ferries to Bute; one from Wemyss
Bay, which is 33 miles (53km) from
Glasgow by car, and one from
Colintraive, which is 75 miles
(121km) from Glasgow.

The ferry from Wemyss Bay sails
to Rothesay and takes about 30
minutes. The smaller summer ferry
from Colintraive sails to Rubodach
on the island's north coast. This
takes about 10 minutes. Operates
early June to Mid August.

Caledonian MacBrayne
Tel: 01475 650100 (general enquiries); 08705 65000 (reservations: charged at BT national long distance rate). Open Monday-Saturday, 0830 to 1700.

Wemyss Bay office (Tel: 01475 520521)

Rothesay office (Tel: 01700 502707); Website: www.calmac.co.uk.

Recorded information for disrupted ferry services Tel: 08457 650050 (charged at local rate).

Getting Around
Bus/coach
Bus services 90 and 490 run from Rothesay to both Kilchattan Bay in the south, Ettrick Bay in the west and Rhubodach (for the Colintraive ferry – schooldays only). The shortened runs between Rothesay and Port Bannatyne are regular (every 30mins) while the longer routes are every couple of hours. The buses also go to Mount Stuart in the summer season.
   Service 489 (schooldays only) links Rothesay and Straad via Ardscalpsie.
   Services 477, 478 and 479 run from Rothesay to Dunoon via Rhubodach Ferry terminal).

Dial-a-bus
On Tuesdays (10:30-14:30) and Saturdays (10:00-16:00) there's a dial-a-bus door-to-door service M107. To book tel: 01546 602869 between 13:15-15:45 on Monday for

Tuesday service, and 13:15-15:00 on Friday for the Saturday service.

Tour bus
Between July and late September, there is also a Grand Island Tour bus from Rothesay Pier, visiting Ascog, Mount Stuart, Kilchattan Bay, Kingarth, Ettrick Bay and Port Bannatyne. (Stagecoach Western Buses). Some tours are on open-top buses.
   The **Isle of Bute Transport Guide** (timetable) is available free of charge from the Tourist Information Centre at Rothesay (Tel: 01700 502151).

Stagecoach Western Buses
Tel: 01700 502076.

Inter-island Cruises
Paddle Steamer cruises aboard the Waverley are undertaken daily in summer with different itineraries each day of the week. From Rothesay the ships visit Millport and the Cumbraes, Brodick, Arran and Holy Island, Pladda, the Kyles of Bute, Tighnabruaich, Loch Fyne and Tarbert.
Contact: Waverley Excursions (Tel: 0141 2432224).

Taxis
S Sweet, 13 Castle Street, Port Bannatyne (Tel: 01700 504000); Sandy Ross, Solway, Serpentine Road, Rothesay (Tel: 01700 504224); A&A Taxis, 56 Ardmory Rd, Rothesay (Tel: 01700 502275); Gaston's Taxis, 21 Argyll Place, Rothesay (Tel: 01700 505050).

Car Hire
No self-drive car hire on the island.

Tourist Information Centres
Discovery Centre, Victoria Street, Rothesay.
Tel: 01700 502151.

Garages/Petrol Stations
W&J Duncan, Mill Street Garage, Rothesay. Tel: 01700 503094.

Bute Motor Company, Union Street, Rothesay. Tel: 01700 502230.

S&B Motors, Union Street, Rothesay. Tel: 01700 505269.

Terry's Auto Repairs, Bishops Street, Rothesay. Tel: 01700 500111/502317.

Rothesay Motor Services, 60 Ladeside Street, Rothesay. Tel: 01700 502045; 01700 504934 (out of hours).

Shops and Post Offices
Ardbeg
Post Office.

Kilchattan Bay
Post Office.

Port Bannatyne
Post office, licensed grocer.

Rothesay
The wide selection of shops include a large Safeway supermarket, 5 Post Offices, stationers, several newsagents, several gifts and souvenir shops, jewellers, tailors (men's and women's), footwear shops, optician, health food, hairdressers, butcher, baker, greengrocer, fishmonger.

Banks
Bank of Scotland, Montague Street, Rothesay.
Tel: 01770 892000. There is a mobile unit in operation.

Royal Bank of Scotland, Victoria Street, Rothesay.
Tel: 01770 30222/302418. There is a mobile unit in operation.

Clydesdale Bank, High Street, Rothesay.
Tel: 01770 503134.

Lloyds TSB Bank, Montague Street, Rothesay.
Tel: 01770 503641.

Hospital
Victoria Hospital, High Street, Rothesay. Tel: 01700 503938.

Doctors' Surgeries
The Bute Practice, The Health Centre, High Street, Rothesay. Tel: 01700 502290.

Dr D T Herriot, 6 Battery Place, Rothesay. Tel: 01700 502388.

Chemist
Bannerman's Pharmacy: 1 Victoria Street, Rothesay. Tel: 01700 502836.

26 Montague Street, Rothesay. Tel 01700 502363.

Dentist
Bute Dental Surgery, 14 West Princes Street, Rothesay. Tel: 01700 502041.

Optician
J B Girkins 18 Tower Street, Rothesay. Tel:01700 504548.

Vetinerary Surgeon
Duncan MacIntyre 17 Argyll Street, Rothesay. Tel: 01700 503017.

Police
High Street, Rothesay. Tel: 01700 502121.

Churches
United Church of Bute (Church of Scotland)
North Bute Church, Port Bannatyne. Tel: 01700 502407.

High Kirk, Upper High Street, Rothesay. Tel: 01700 502407.

Kingarth and Kilchattan Bay Church, Kilchattan Bay. Tel: 01700 502407.

Roman Catholic Church
St Andrew's, Bridgend Street, Rothesay. Tel: 01700 502047.

Scottish Episcopal Church (Anglican)
St Paul's, Victoria Street, Rothesay. Tel: 01369 702972.

Trinity Church, Castle Street, Rothesay. Tel: 01700 502797.

Ardbeg Baptist Church
King Street, Ardbeg.

Rothesay Christian Fellowship
Bishop Street, Rothesay.
Details of all Bute's church services appear each week in *The Buteman*.

Maps
Ordnance Survey
Ordnance Survey Explorer 362 Cowal and Isle of Bute.
1:25000 scale and superb for walkers
Ordnance Survey Landranger 63 Firth of Clyde.
1:50000 scale a good touring map and it includes the Cumbraes and Ayrshire Coast.

Practical Information: Great Cumbrae

Getting There
By air
The nearest airport is Prestwick, which is 30 miles (43km) from the ferry terminal at Largs. Prestwick has flights to and from Ireland, the rest of the UK and Europe.

Ryanair operate budget flights to it from London Stanstead. ScotRail have special offers for rail travellers flying in to Prestwick.

Glasgow International Airport is 22 miles (36km) from Largs, while Glasgow city centre is 32 miles (51km).

Glasgow Prestwick Airport.
Website: www.gpia.co.uk.

Ryanair.
Website: www.ryanair.com.

By rail

There is a regular connecting rail service from Glasgow Central to Largs (for ferry).

ScotRail

Contacts: All rail enquiries: 08457 48 49 50; Website: www.scotrail.co.uk; ScotRail Telesales: Tel: 08457 550033.

By ferry

You catch the Caledonian MacBrayne ferry to Great Cumbrae at Largs. It takes 10 minutes to get to Cumbrae Slip. If you're on foot there's a bus (it's always there to meet you) that takes you to Millport. Sailings are every 15 minutes in summer and 30 minutes at other times. Last check-in 5 minutes before departure.

Caledonian MacBrayne

Tel: 01475 650100 (general enquiries); 08705 65000 (reservations) charged at BT national long distance rate. Open: Monday-Saturday, 0830 and 1700. Largs office (Tel: 01475 674134). Website: www.calmac.co.uk.

Recorded information for disrupted ferry services Tel: 08457 650050 (charged at local rate).

On your own boat

There are plenty of good moorings at Millport. No charge is levied. There are pontoons and about a dozen buoys just off the pier.

Getting Around
Bus/coach

The only bus operating is the one that takes you from the slip in the north of the island to Millport, but then Great Cumbrae's rather small. There's also an open-top bus tour.

Inter-island Paddle Steamer Cruises

Paddle Steamer cruises aboard the Waverley are undertaken daily in summer with different itineraries each day of the week. They include visits to Rothesay, Dunoon, Largs, Millport, Brodick, and around Ailsa Craig.
Contact: Waverley Excursions. Tel: 0141 243 2224.

Taxis

Contact: Caldwell's Newsagent, Millport. Tel: 01475 530443.

Tourist Information Centre

28 Stuart Street, Millport.
Tel/fax: 01475 530753; Email: info@millport.org.

Garages/ Petrol Stations

R K Horn Ritchie Street, Millport (repairs, 24-hour breakdown and recovery). Tel: 01475 530567.

County Garage 1 Marine Parade, Millport (fuel). Tel: 01475 530682.

Self Drive Car Hire

None on the island.

Shops and Post Offices
Millport

Supermarket, butcher, cycle hire, newsagent, card & gift shop, hair stylist,

Banks
Bank of Scotland, 42 Stuart Street, Millport.
Tel: 01475 531073.

Hospital
Lady Margaret Hospital. Tel: 01475 530307.

Doctors' Surgeries
Drs J & E Bryson, 10 Kelburn Street, Millport. Tel: 01475 530329.

Chemist
There is no pharmacy on the island. Prescriptions are dispensed by the surgery doctors.

Dentist
Nearest at Largs
WPG Mitchell, 26 Wilson Street, Largs. Tel: 01475 672009.

Jamieson and Brown, 46 Main Street, Largs. Tel: 01475 672009.

Optician
Nearest at Largs
D Bonellie 101 Main Street, Largs. Tel: 01475 674553.

Opticare Opticians, 8 Aitken Street, Largs. Tel: 01475 673985.

Veterinary Surgeon
Nearest at Largs
The Oaks Vetinerary Centre, 2 George Street, Largs. Tel: 01475 673644.

Police
Police Station. Tel: 01475 530316.

Churches
Church of Scotland
Cumbrae Parish Church. Tel: 01475 530416.

Scottish Episcopal Church (Anglican)
Cathedral of the Isles. Tel: 01475 530353.

Presbyterian
Church of Our Lady of Perpetual Succour Presbytery. Tel: 01475 530537.

Maps
Ordnance Survey
Ordnance Survey Explorer 341 Greenock, Largs & Millport
1:25 000 scale and superb for walkers
Ordnance Survey Landranger 63 Firth of Clyde
1:50 000 scale a good all round map and it includes the Isle of Bute, Ayrshire Coast, Dunoon and Greenock

Visiting Little Cumbrae
Little Cumbrae is a privately owned island. It is up for sale in 2002, and things could change, so check with the Tourist Information Centre (address below). For the present permission can be obtained from Little Cumbrae Estates Ltd., PO Box 1, Millport, Great Cumbrae, North Ayrshire KA28 0AA, or Robert Reid, Largs (Tel: 01294 601844).

Bibliography

General

Arran and the Clyde Islands. British Geological Survey – a very good insight into the region's geology
Arran and Bute. Christine Weiner (S Forsyth) – very informative history of the two islands
The Lords of the Isles. Ronald Williams (House of Lochar) – a detailed look at the Clan Donald
Scottish Island Hopping. (Polygon)

Arran

The Isle of Arran. Robert McLellan (David & Charles) – out of print but worth the search
The Isle of Arran. Robert McLellan (Pevensey Island Guide) – good photos
The Arran Flora. Tony Church and Tony Smith (Arran Natural History Society) – a good check list
History of the Villages of the Isle of Arran. Scottish Womens' Rural Institute Arran
Walking in Arran. Paddy Dillon (Cicerone Press)

Bute

The Isle of Bute. Ian S Munro (David & Charles) – out of print but worth the search
The Isle of Bute. Norman Newton (Pevensey Island Guide) – good photos
The History of Bute. Dorothy N Marshall (self published) – fascinating read
Nature Trails. 5 booklets – Buteshire Natural History Society
The Isle of Bute. Map Guide to Eight Easy to Follow Walks (Footprint)
The West Island Way. (Footprint)

Cumbrae

Millport and the Cumbraes, a History and Guide. J R D Campbell (Cunninghame District Council) – unobtainable at time of writing but very authoritative.

Index

Acknowledgements

Many people have helped me with this book and I would like to than them all. The Tourist Information staff at both Rothesay and Brodick couldn't have been more helpful, and Dr Jim Bryson at the Tourist Information Centre in Millport spent more time than I could have reasonably asked getting me the most up to date data on the island of Cumbrae. Thanks also to Caledonian-MacBrayne for sailing me across to the islands – on time, every time – and to all the friendly people I have met on my trips.